# ECONOMIC RATIONALITY AND PRACTICAL REASON

# THEORY AND DECISION LIBRARY

*General Editors:* W. Leinfellner (*Vienna*) and G. Eberlein (*Munich*)

Series A: Philosophy and Methodology of the Social Sciences

Series B: Mathematical and Statistical Methods

Series C: Game Theory, Mathematical Programming and Operations Research

Series D: System Theory, Knowledge Engineering and Problem Solving

## SERIES A: PHILOSOPHY AND METHODOLOGY OF THE SOCIAL SCIENCES

VOLUME 24



*Scope:* This series deals with the foundations, the general methodology and the criteria, goals and purpose of the social sciences. The emphasis in the Series A will be on well-argued, thoroughly analytical rather than advanced mathematical treatments. In this context, particular attention will be paid to game and decision theory and general philosophical topics from mathematics, psychology and economics, such as game theory, voting and welfare theory, with applications to political science, sociology, law and ethics.

*The titles published in this series are listed at the end of this volume.*

# ECONOMIC RATIONALITY AND PRACTICAL REASON

*by*

JULIAN NIDA-RÜMELIN
*Georg-August Universität,
Göttingen, Germany*

KLUWER ACADEMIC PUBLISHERS
DORDRECHT / BOSTON / LONDON

A C.I.P. Catalogue record for this book is available from the Library of Congress

ISBN 0-7923-4493-6

Published by Kluwer Academic Publishers,
P.O. Box 17, 3300 AA Dordrecht, The Netherlands.

Kluwer Academic Publishers incorporates
the publishing programmes of
D. Reidel, Martinus Nijhoff, Dr W. Junk and MTP Press.

Sold and distributed in the U.S.A. and Canada
by Kluwer Academic Publishers,
101 Philip Drive, Norwell, MA 02061, U.S.A.

In all other countries, sold and distributed
by Kluwer Academic Publishers Group,
P.O. Box 322, 3300 AH Dordrecht, The Netherlands.

*Printed on acid-free paper*



Printed in the Netherlands

# Contents

# Preface

The theory of practical rationality does not belong to one academic discipline alone. There are quite divergent philosophical, economical, sociological, psychological and politological contributions. Sometimes the disciplinary boundaries impede theoretical progress. On the other hand it is an indication for the high complexity of the subject that so many divergent paradigms compete with one another, or - what is worse - live separately in a kind of splendid isolation.

Decision theory in the broader sense, embracing the theory of games and collective choice theory, can help to understand practical reason in philosophical analysis. But there are interesting aspects which cannot be dealt with adequately within a decision-theoretic conceptual framework. To have both of these convictions justifies to neglect disciplinary boundaries and poses a problem for the orthodoxies of either sides.

All the essays of this volume focus on the relation between economic rationality and practical reason and discuss different aspects of the same problem, i. e. a basic deficiency in the standard economic theory of practical rationality. But philosophical analysis would not be of much help if it just rejected the economic paradigm. It must rather help to integrate economic aspects into a broader view on practical reason.

The first chapter was read in German to the conference "Norms, Values and Society" organized by the Institute Vienna Circle in October 1993. The English version appeared in the proceedings (ed. by H. Pauer-Studer (1994)). The second chapter was read as an introductory lecture of a workshop on rational choice in October 1991, published in the proceedings *Praktische Rationalität*, ed. by the author (1994). An English translation by Hanjo Glock was published in *Ratio* (New Series) 7 (1994). Chapter 8 originally appeared in *Theory and Decision* 30 (1991). A German version of chapter 9 has been published in *Protosoziologie* 6 (1994). Chapters 3, 4 and 10 are based on the chapters 2, 3, 14 and 15 of my *Kritik des Konsequentialismus*. Chapter

5 is based on §§ 2 and 3 of my *Entscheidungstheorie und Ethik*. The basic idea of chapter 7 has been developed in § 7 and in the appendix of *Entscheidungstheorie und Ethik*. The text is part of an article which enriches this idea with some mathematical results written together with Thomas Schmidt and Axel Munk, published in *Theory and Decision* 41 (1996).

The chapters dealing with different but related aspects of the same problem are sufficiently self-contained to be read separately and independently. To allow this kind of reading which the hasty reader might prefer, I refrained from removing overlapping parts and repetitions of arguments.

I am grateful to Dagmar Mirbach for providing English drafts of parts of the manuscript, Thomas Schmidt for collecting and carefully revising the whole manuscript and adding new English translations to it, and Werner Leinfellner, who - knowing my German work on the subject - proposed to publish some of my results in this series. The permissions by the publishers to use material published before for this volume are gratefully acknowledged.

Göttingen in November 1996
JNR

## CHAPTER 1

# Rationality and Morality

### 1. The Unity of the Normative 'Ought'

'If an action is immoral, one ought not to carry it out.' This thesis is one of those elements of our belief system which we are under normal circumstances unwilling to revise. 'If an action is irrational, one ought not to carry it out.' This second thesis is less cogent. It is possible that a person faced with the alternative of performing the action $a$ or the action $a'$ ought to carry out $a$ for moral reasons even if $a$ is irrational for her (i. e. does not correspond to her goals). The person-relativity of rationality of actions seems to be responsible for this difference. An action is rational in relation to the personal wishes of that person. The conclusion is eventually: we are dealing with two normative theories, one of which determines what is moral, the other what is rational. Both contain specific prescriptions: one should be both - moral and rational - as far as this is possible; in case of conflict the two norms must be weighed against one another. The pure universalist will give precedence to morality in case of a conflict; the radical particularist will favour rationality. My claim instead is: there can be only one normative theory; thus this conflict between two normative criteria or types of criteria is merely imaginary. To illustrate this I will tell an odd story which may seem familiar to some of the readers:

Uncle Charles, an elderly, wealthy bachelor and Fred, his nephew and sole heir, are sitting in a small fishing boat. The water is alive with sharks. No other boat is in sight. The following dialogue develops:

*Fred:* You know, I would do anything to get my hands on half a million dollars with which to finance my pleasures.

*Uncle Charles:* I know you well enough to believe that. After all, lately you have tried out a lot of ways of getting money, all of which have failed.

*Fred:* That's right. In fact, in the meantime I have come to believe that there is only one way for me to get my hands on so much money, and that is to kill you.

*Uncle Charles:* I am afraid that with your limited abilities and indolent tendencies there is indeed no other way for you to get the money you desire.

*Fred:* If you admit that there is no other way for me to get this money, what advice do you give me?

*Uncle Charles:* Since you have only one wish - to get your hands on some quick money - and there is no other way to fulfill this wish apart from killing me, you should push me out of the boat.

*Fred:* I agree with both of your premises and your conclusion and, since I have always followed the good advice of my uncle, I will now push you out of the boat. (Fred pushes Uncle Charles out of the boat.)

R.M. Hare told this story in an article from 1971 entitled "Wanting - Some Pitfalls".[1] It served other purposes in that context, however.

An interpretation according to the two normative criteria is almost irresistible. According to it, we are here confronted with a conflict between rationality and morality. It would be admittedly rational for Fred to push Uncle Charles out of the boat, but at the same time this action would be immoral. Here, in any case, morality has precedence. Therefore, it follows that Fred should not push Uncle Charles out of the boat.

Both the intentional (cognitive, preferential) premise - Fred has the dominating *desire* to get his hands on some money - and the epistemic premise - Fred *knows* that there is no other way for him to get his hands on some money - may be true, so that it is undeniably accurate to say that it lies in Fred's interest to push his uncle out of the boat - and nevertheless the conclusion - 'Fred should push his uncle out of the boat' - is not valid. Both premises do not suffice for this conclusion. It might of course be possible for one of Fred's friends sharing his attitu-

[1] In Brinkley (1971). Hare argues in this article against Black for the so-called Hume's Law; see also Black (1964).

de of mind to recommend - on the basis of the facts these premises establish - that he kills his uncle. Yet, then, something remarkable takes place: with this recommendation the friend has 'identified' himself to some degree with Fred's goals.

Uncle Charles would make no mistake (or at least no logical one) by identifying both premises as being empirically accurate without accepting the conclusion. In order to escape the snares of linguistic vagueness, Uncle Charles could answer: 'I do not doubt that both assumptions hold. Thus, I know that you can achieve your goal only by pushing me out of the boat. Yet, I do not believe you should pursue your goals under these circumstances. Therefore, I also do not believe that you should push me out of the boat.' If, however, Uncle Charles - despite the negative effects it would have for him - believes that Fred should pursue his goals even under these circumstances (Uncle Charles might believe, e. g., that his life is nearing an end, whereas he does not see any other opportunity for Fred to improve his situation), then Uncle Charles could concur with his nephew's conclusion.

When - on the basis of his knowledge of the subjective goals and the feasible options - the speaker supports the action (and advises the other to carry out the action) which optimizes these goals, he is exhibiting at the same time a certain pro-attitude. This attitude must not be confused with the speaker's sharing the goals of the person advised; he does not have to make the latter's goals his own. He might personally pursue completely different goals. The pro-attitude applies to the involved person's pursuing and reaching her goals.

The talk of equal goals is rather unclear here anyway, since the goals of a person's actions are usually self-referential. The person does not want anything; rather, he wants to accomplish something. Intentions preceding an action are usually, perhaps always, self-referential, motivating intentions.[2] If both Heitmann and Rau want to become Germany's Federal President, then they do not have the same, but rather different goals. Heitmann wants Heitmann to become president, and Rau wants Rau to become president. Both goals thus cannot be simultaneously fulfilled. If Heitmann wants Rau to become president and Heitmann to remain Saxony's Minister of the Interior, then he would probably have the same goals that Rau at present seems to have. There can be interpersonally equal preferences insofar as individual

[2] See also ch. 3 below.

rankings of states of affairs agree with one another, but not all preferences are action guiding. Preferences which become action guiding intentions (or which instruct these) are usually self-referential.

Now observe the following case. A person actually says after hearing this story that 'Fred ought to push Uncle Charles out of the boat.' We are amazed and ask him whether he considers such an action to be morally defensible. He answers 'No'. Cases of this kind occur without doubt frequently in every-day situations: someone advocates an action because it is in the interest of the person carrying out the action and says at the same time that this action is not morally correct. This seems to reinforce once more the idea of the two normative criteria - on the one hand the one of rationality, on the other the one of morality. This is plausible, however, only upon superficial analysis. We can ascertain this through appropriate inquiries into moral every-day language. We will ask the persons what they mean when they say that this action is immoral. They might then answer that this action is not consistent with the moral convictions of most people or they might make clear through other formulations that they do not mean this apparently moral verdict to be normative. However, these inquiries might also prove that the 'ought' answer was not meant to be normative - which Hare discusses as a 'non-separable ought'. My thesis suggests in any case that at least one of the two claims - '*a* is rational' and '*a* is immoral' - is being used by this person in a non-normative sense. There is only one normative assessment for which, however, a variety of parameters is relevant: among other things interests, institutions and that which Hegelians and Aristotelians like to call 'Sittlichkeit'. Put briefly, *there is only one normative obligation.*

## 2. The Theory of Practical Rationality as a Theory of Good Reasons

Instead of saying, 'You should not do *a*', one could also say, 'There is no good reason for your doing *a*'. Thus, the theory of practical rationality can be constructed as a theory of good reasons for action. At least since the beginning of the modern age, all philosophical theories of practical rationality are to a large extent reductivist. According to them, the variety of reasons for actions is only an illusion; in reality there is only one principle (only one rule and criterion) which decides whether an action is rational. One must take this claim seriously. If *P* is the appropriate principle or criterion, then it must follow that one must be able to *rationally reconstruct* every good reason for action with the assistance of $P$. The action $a$ is rational if $a$ fulfills $P$. If this theory is adequate, then for every reason $R$ for an action $a$ it must hold: if $a$ is well justified by $R$, then $a$ must fulfill $P$. This is a strong assumption and however $P$ might be defined - *prima facie* little seems to speak for the assumption that $P$ could fulfill this condition.

At dinner my neighbour asks me for the salt. I pass it to her. It is not very probable that someone will ask me why I did this. Should someone ask me, however, I would have a prompt answer: I passed her the salt because she requested it. The fact that I was asked to do $a$ is under normal circumstances a good reason for doing $a$.

$P$ is the principle of optimizing the subjective consequences of one's actions. There remains much to be said to make this principle precise[3], e. g. that it is compatible with a theory about how to evaluate this result rationally and morally. Yet, even without specifying it further, it seems that already this simple example of a good reason balks against a reconstruction through $P$. Under normal circumstances a request is a good reason for its fulfillment. Under normal circumstances this reason is sufficient and it requires no further justification. Especially the consequences (and my subjective evaluation of them) seem to be irrelevant. I have a good reason to act according to this request, even if I should think that low-sodium cuisine is more healthy. In any case, I do not have a good reason for passing the salt only if I suppose that the causal and probable consequences of this action are optimal. If I answer the question of why I passed the salt with a consideration regarding the consequences of this action (i. e. I take $P$ as the criterion of practical rationality), then this would under normal conditions be considered discourteous to the person having made this request, as I apparently did not accept her request as a genuine reason for action (it must not be the sufficient or primary reason for this action). Her request would have been just one of the empirical conditions taken into consideration. This argument taken by itself is not a refutation of $P$. Yet, if it is true that making a request under certain conditions can represent a good reason for fulfilling this request *and* that fulfilling this request has less than optimal results in some of

---

[3] Cf. Nida-Rümelin (1993b), §§ 1-14. See also ch. 2, 4 and 5 below.

these cases, then the principle $P$ - we can call it the consequentialist principle - runs into difficulties.

I would, however, like to rule out a possible misunderstanding: this notion of the theory of practical rationality as a theory of good reasons does not mean a commitment to institutional ethics. This latter conception of ethics, which is founded on speech act theory, claims to overcome the logical gap between 'Is' and 'Ought'. E. g., the institution of promising constitutes certain expectations: if person A says to person B, 'I will pay you back the money I owe you tomorrow', then A has obliged himself through this promise of paying back the money the next day. Under normal circumstances there is an obligation to do *a* for A (because A promised). The validity of the statement 'A is obliged to do *a*' can be proven - seemingly - through the mere recourse to the empirical contents (A made the statement to B under such and such conditions, B must have understood this to be a promise, A knew that B..., etc.) and - without the assistance of normative criteria - a normative statement seems to be deducable from exclusively descriptive premises.[4] A certain normative quality seems inherent to institutions. This 'overcoming' of the naturalistic fallacy which is characteristical for the different approaches of institutional ethics has a weakness, however. It disregards the fact that the assumed normativity of institutions (or, at least, of certain institutions) can also be interpreted descriptively. I can describe the *de facto* existence of normative rules without actually sharing them. I can place myself outside of this framework (taking an ethnological point of view) and not attach any subjectively shared prescriptions to the ascertainment of normative contents.[5] The theory of the naturalistic fallacy *and* the theory of institutional facts including their normative constitutive conditions are not thereby violated.

It is a good reason to do something because someone else requested it to be done. This seems to be accurate not only *empirically*, as a component of an *internal* description of an institutional fact, but also *normatively* - thus the qualification of the reason for the action as 'good'. If someone can persuade me that it is in my personal interest to generally fulfill the requests of other persons and when this entails no further disadvantages, this may strengthen my conviction that some-

---

[4] See also Searle (1969), ch. 8.

[5] See also Mackie (1977), ch. 3.

one's request itself provides a good reason to fulfill this request; yet, this information does not substitute my conviction that a request provides a good reason to act.

Someone asks you why you just did this, *a*, and not that, *a*', and you answer, 'Under the given circumstances I considered *a* to be my (moral) duty'.[6] The question, 'Why be moral', is superfluous. The fact that something is morally required or desirable is considered to be a sufficient reason for action under normal circumstances, or, formulated internally: the conviction that *a* is morally required is a good (internal) reason for *a*. Here the method of philosophical doubting seems to have reached its limits drawn by central elements of our belief system. The appropriate philosophical answer to the question, 'Why be moral', is a theory of practical rationality which shows that the moral is also rational.

## 3. Philosophical Explanations of Morality

There are three paradigmatic philosophical conceptions of the relationship of practical rationality and morality.

### a. Personal Advantage

The first conception is that of the *Gorgias* dialogue. A person should be moral because it is personally advantageous to be moral. This agreement of personal interest and moral imperative, if it were in fact to be proven, would have the great advantage to be a lucid theory of individual rationality (the optimization of one's own advantage) explaining with unquestionably motivating character the conducive demands of moral judgement. For Plato, this proof is indispensable for the refutation of the sophistic argumentation. If the sophists were able to show that it is not in one's personal interest to be moral (*dikaios*),

---

[6] Today most people avoid this moralizing vocabulary and would express the same conviction using a different language. They might say: 'It was most likely necessary to do that' or 'I could not have acted differently, considering the situation he is in', that is to say, they would like to stress the subjective character of their moral conviction or represent their convictions as dispositional influence. This should not, however, hide the fact that even in these statements the conviction that something is *morally necessary* or *morally correct* is seen as a good reason for action.

then it would look bad indeed for the conducive character of moral judgement. Socrates' argumentation in the *Gorgias* is, however, not convincing at this point. The thesis that it is better to suffer wrong than to do wrong and worse to do wrong and go unpunished than to do wrong and be punished for it - where 'better' and 'worse' are interpreted in the sense of personal advantage - must get involved in less than convincing psychological speculations. Yet, it goes beyond that. The notion that a just punishment benefits the soul and that it therefore cannot lie in one's self-interest to evade a just punishment reflects - like the re-assuring hypothesis of a compensatory justice after the end of life on earth - a more complex concept of self-interest which ends up in the theory of the structural harmony of the just soul and lastly in the theory of forms. The contemporary variations of Socrates' congruence thesis in the *Gorgias* dialogue can be seen in the recent attempts in decision theory of modelling interpersonal cooperation as an expression of individual optimization of interests in iterated prisoners' dilemma games.[7]

b. Establishment

The second paradigmatic understanding of the relation of practical rationality and morality is that of Thomas Hobbes.[8] Humans individually optimize their interests. This optimization does not, however, lead to a stable model of societal cooperation, but rather to a war of everyone against everyone. The natural differences in strength and ability do not suffice for the establishment of a natural hierarchy. Yet, as a rationally optimizing being, man knows precisely which rules of interaction he must follow in order to end the *status naturalis* and to establish a condition of peace. These rules are well-founded as they are in the interest of all: a general compliance with them by everyone entails a greater advantage for each person than a general non-compliance. These rules - ironically called by Hobbes 'laws of nature' (*leges naturales*) -

---

[7] See Axelrod (1984) and Hegselmann (1993). The results of these and other computer simulations are often interpreted in the literature as a proof of the libertarian thesis of the harmony of individually optimizing action in self-interest and social cooperation. An exact analysis reveals, however, that sweeping conclusions of this sort are not justified; see Kondo (1990) and Schüssler (1990).

[8] See: *De Homine* (1658), esp. ch. 11-13; *De Cive* (1642, 1647), esp. ch. 1-4, and *Leviathan* (1651), esp. ch. 13-15.

nonetheless have no conducive function in *statu naturale*, for, although they are in the common interest, an individual compliance with them does not serve individual interests: *ceteris paribus* it is better for each individual not to follow the rules. Since Hobbes' conception of rationality assumes the individual optimization of interest as a criterion, however, behaviour orientates itself on the law of nature (*ius naturale*): everything which seems to serve one's personal interests is allowed. There is no good reason to adhere to these rules of cooperation, although the general compliance with them by everyone would serve my own interests, too. These rules could only be conducive if an option presented itself, whereby the conditions of behaviour were so transformed that in the future it would serve both the common as well as the individual interest to follow the laws of nature. This option exists: it is the act of a general disarmament and the transfer of all power to a central authority. Whereas, with Hobbes, morality is established by creating a practical monopoly of power, contemporary Hobbesian variations extend the concept through the creation of moral rules in other forms (socialisation, sanctions *in foro interno*, etc.). Hobbesian ethics answers the question 'Why be moral?' by a reference to established and sanctioned rules. The fact that rules are founded on reason cannot alone give sufficient justification for following these rules. Only with their factual establishment does a good reason for adhering to them appear.

### c. Practical Reason

The third paradigmatic understanding of the relation between practical rationality and morality was provided by Immanuel Kant.[9] According to Kant, the heart of morality is constituted by the assumption that man is a rational being. In as much as he is a rational being, his subjective behavioural motives (*maxims*) are subject to a test of their rationality: the general application of the maxims must not lead to *incoherence*. Self-defeating is the most stringent variation of incoherence: maxims the general application of which is undesirable for a person are irrational, *a fortiori* so are maxims whose general effectiveness is *logically impossible*. This compatibility test of maxims in the 'realm of reasons'

[9] See: *Grundlegung zur Metaphysik der Sitten* (1785); *Die Metaphysik der Sitten* (1797); *Kritik der praktischen Vernunft* (1788), esp. 1. Part, 1. B., First and Third Main Sections.

marks three concentric areas of morality: logical incompatibility constitutes what is *unconditionally morally forbidden* ('absolute duties'); voluntary incompatibility constitutes what is *conditionally morally forbidden* (non-absolute duties); and the altruistic consideration of the desires of others constitutes *supererogative moral actions*. The moral duties are expressions of the autonomy of reason. The question 'Why be moral?' is answered in the following way: only he who gives himself the 'laws' of his behaviour is free. The legal nature (universal coherence) of the autonomous will contains, however, at the same time those limits which constitute the morality of a person. Rational behaviour is behaviour proceeding from the consciousness of one's own autonomy (from 'respect for the moral law').

## 4. Structural Rationality

While these three paradigmatic philosophical answers to the question 'Why be moral?' are - each taken by itself - insufficient, each refers at the same time to an essential aspect of a satisfactory answer. These aspects shall be sketched in the following.

### a. Self-interest

A group of persons, who individually optimize their personal interests, does not generally optimize the personal interests of these persons. If each individual person $i$ from the group $G$ ($i=1, 2,..., n$) chooses the same strategy $s(i)$, which has for her - personally - the best consequences, it can nonetheless be the case that the combination of these individual strategies $[s(1), s(2), s(3),..., s(n)]$ is disadvantageous for herself as well as for all others, i. e. that there is another combination of individual strategies $[s^*(1), s^*(2), s^*(3),..., s^*(n)]$ which for all persons $i$ from $G$ would be more advantageous: the combination of strategies is *collectively irrational*. The much-discussed prisoners' dilemma is paradigmatic for this kind of situation. Individual optimization leads from time to time to collectively irrational results. This does not apply when the interaction in the group takes place under the conditions of the ideal, competitive market. It is for this reason that many economists as well as many moral philosophers consider the market to be a morally free zone.[10]

Persons exclusively interested in the optimization of their own advantage (i. e. 'rational egotists') thus have an interest in other persons' adherence to moral rules which limit the latter's individual optimization of interests. The most advantageous situation prevails when everyone adheres to certain moral rules except oneself; the second best situation when everyone complies with the rules including oneself; the third best when no one follows the moral rules; and the worst situation when no one adheres to the rules except oneself. There is, therefore, an individual incentive for the egotistical rationalist not to adhere to the moral rules. On the other hand, the rational egotist will not publicly argue for everyone not to comply with the rules, as this might actually inspire someone not to comply with them, which would not be in the interest of the rational egotist.

Even at this first general characterization of the conflict between individual and collective rationality an interesting aspect becomes obvious: the rational egotist is forced into a certain incoherence. He cannot say what he believes to be correct. Inasmuch as his behaviour is transparent, i. e. shows some information on his convictions and could lead others to behave according to these convictions, he cannot optimize his interests directly, but rather only in consideration of this incentive effect. Indeed, one can imagine empirical conditions under which the rational egotist would be mutated to a pure moralist without having abandoned his original behavioural motivation.

This consideration can be expanded to a more principal observation. If there is a good reason $R$ to do $a$, then the acting person justifies $a$ to others by referring to $R$. A radically individualistic conception - like the standard interpretation of decision theory - relativizes the rationality of an action to subjective desirability and subjective belief. Interestingly, our normative everyday language forbids such a stark subjectivity. The grammar of the use of 'ought' rules out such a radical subjectivity.

Imagine that a person A pursues certain subjective goals and estimates the likelihood of the relevant conditions in a way letting the action $a$ appear rational according to the decision-theoretic criterion of optimization. The normative interpretation of this criterion says that

---

[10] See Gauthier (1986), ch. 4.

this person *ought*, assuming he indeed has these subjective wishes and beliefs, to do *a*. This 'ought' might be irreconcilable with the moral convictions of other persons, of B e. g.; nonetheless, a certain weak sense of 'ought' can still exist, since B believes that A should do *a*. This could be made plausible in the following way: B wishes to be sure that A would pursue other, e. g. more morally acceptable goals, yet, in view of A's actual goals, *a* is the rational action for A, and B believes, consequently, that A ought to do *a*. B would, however, rather like A to have other goals which would be reached through other actions. In this sense, B would prefer A to behave differently. B is in no way incoherent in this desire. His moral convictions voice themselves in a preference for A developping other preferences. B takes up a supportive position vis à vis A's preferences only inasmuch as he supports their fulfillment. Yet, B would prefer A to have other preferences; in this sense, B does not support the existing preferences. The support necessary for a normative 'ought' which I mentioned in the first section thus refers to the fulfillment of given preferences and not to the given preferences themselves.

Good reasons for action thus have a logically compulsory *intersubjective* component. Reasons for action which are not suitable for justifying an action to other persons are not good reasons for action. The optimization of one's own advantage constitutes a good reason for an action only within the boundaries of an intersubjective criterion of permissible and defensible actions and goals. A boundary which every plausible intersubjective criterion will define is that of collective irrationality. Where the optimization of one's own advantage is collectively irrational, it cannot constitute a good reason for action.

### b. Establishment

Mere conventions, i. e. rules which can claim no 'moral dignity' for themselves, influence nonetheless moral reasons for an action. At many religious sites certain clothing regulations are valid, and the moral obligation of these regulations fulfillment also applies to those which do not share the respective religious orientation. This moral obligation can be made plausible - independent of any religious orientation - with the universal moral principle of showing consideration and respect towards dissenters. Relativist metatheories of morality move the rôle of moral reasons for an action towards reasons for mere conventional actions.

Cognitivist versions of relativism thus identify the morally necessary with culturally established values (realistic contextualism). Non-cognitivist versions of relativism consider the notion of a moral cognition to be misleading: criteria for what is right and wrong cannot be applied to moral convictions, since their application implies an objective standpoint, which cannot exist because of the radical contextuality of moral norms.[11]

For a universalist and cognitivist conception of ethics, the factual establishment of moral norms is not at all irrelevant for two reasons. First, ethical principles - whatever their content - must be transferred into norms which can have a directly conducive effect. This placing in concrete terms must generally take reference to contingent empirical conditions of application, to which the respective cultural frame belongs. Practice norms can to a large extent vary between cultures without risking cut-backs on the universalist claim of ethical norms.[12]

Secondly, the moral relevance of the established moral rules can be explained by the *underdetermination* of collective rationality. A central area of morality can be reconstructed as a system of norms of interaction, which should secure collective rationality (or formulated in decision-theoretic terms which exclude Pareto-dominated collective actions). Often there is a variety of possibilities for achieving this. If one takes into account the combination of norms of interaction and the limited flexibility and malleability of human agents, then this potential variety is reduced. Conventions can be understood as a more or less arbitrary restriction to one or a few of these possibilities. Their establishment makes them morally relevant even when they themselves are indifferent under moral aspects.

---

11 See Harmann (1982) and Arrington (1989).

12 An easily remembered example is offered by the different variations of contemporary preference utilitarianism. Whereas the ethical principle of the maximization of preference fulfillment claims unlimited universal validity, the respective practical norms to be applied could to a large extend depend on the closer empirical conditions, the cognitive competence of the acting persons, the cultural orientations of the affected society, the dispositional influence of individual wishes, etc. See, for example, J. J. C. Smart's argumentation in Smart/Williams (1973); Hare's concept of the 'intuitive level of moral thinking', in: Hare (1981), esp. pp. 44-64, and Dieter Birnbacher's 'Praxisnormen', in Birnbacher (1988), esp. ch. 6.

### c. Coherence

Let us turn once more to the self-interested person. A primary problem of coherence arises in the tension between self-oriented optimization of interests on the one hand and the moral point of view on the other. The rational egotist must publicly promote the general compliance with moral norms and privately break these norms from time to time. The more transparent his own behavioural orientation is, the more probable it will be that the rational egotist will wish in his own interest to be a moralist. The tendency of rational egotists to interact with cooperative persons rather than with uncooperative ones can (under favourable conditions) lead to the establishment of moral rules from solely egotistically rational interaction. Very often these favourable conditions are not fulfilled and thus the question 'Why be moral' cannot be answered positively on the basis of a congruence between self-interest and morality.

A person's coherence encompasses among other things an agreement between his convictions and actions. Inherent to good reason for action is its potential publicity. This potential publicity of good reasons places tight restrictions on a person's possible moral reasons (whether these restrictions suffice to determine the content of moral principles - as several rationalist moral philosophers assume[13] - may remain open). What is decisive is the fact that the complex of moral reasons has a conducive effect due to the close connection between individual convictions and individual behaviour. A person cannot morally disapprove of certain societal behavioural patterns and personally act in a way reflecting the constitutive elements of these societal behavioural patterns. The 'cannot' of the last sentence marks something weaker than logical impossibility. He 'can' very well in singular cases, but not repeatedly and generally without becoming unreliable as a person. Actions are, if not logical *constitutiva*, then at least *indicativa* of propositional attitudes. This attribution of a propositional attitude does not occur primarily on the basis of *verbally expressed* attitudes. A person is characterized by complexes of attitudes, dispositions, behavioural patterns, expressions, etc., which are in a close, reciprocal dependent relation-

---

[13] See Gewirth (1978) and the reconstruction of this approach by Klaus Steigleder in his (1992).

ship to one another. The unity of a person requires a certain coherence of these interconnected complexes.

A person attempting to optimize pointwise would fall to pieces and appear incoherent and incomprehensible. A society the members of which optimize individually would become incoherent and make collective rationality in general (individual) interest impossible. Persons are capable of choosing actions in view of comprehensive structures. Naming reasons for an action means nothing more than relating to a comprehensive structure, to the *constitutiva* of which the appropriate action belongs. These structures can consist in types of actions, but also in allocations of individual rights, in general rules of co-operation or even in mere attitudes (respect, compassion, etc.). A structure $S$ approved by the acting person is a good reason for $a$, if $a$ belongs to the *constitutiva* of $S$. Structures are approved because they - for their part - are *constitutiva* of more comprehensive structures which are likewise approved. The comprehensive structures might, on the other hand, be approved exactly because they contain attractive sub-structures. Coherence does not develop from the general to the concrete. We have stable moral convictions, both in relation to individual concrete actions and in relation to the most comprehensive structural characteristics (like fairness). The ethical theory goes forward and backward - from the general to the concrete and vice versa - with the goal of constructing theoretical coherence, a coherence of our ethical judgements. Theoretical coherence as a methodological orientation of ethics represents therein an essential part of practical coherence, which represents itself in actions, expressions and attitudes. Moral reasons for an action are related primarily to rules which guarantee the societal (collective) rationality, but they also have the function of making intrapersonal coherence possible ('duties against oneself' in the Kantian terminology, the theory of the 'good life' in Aristotelian terms). Rationality understood in this broader, structural sense, covers an essential part of morality. At least for this part it is valid to claim: it is rational to be moral.

CHAPTER 2

# Rational Choice: Extensions and Revisions

## 1. The Basic Model

A person acts rationally if her actions appear to make sense with respect to the person's aims. Actions make sense with respect to a person's aims if they seem to be appropriate means for achieving those aims.

These two propositions constitute the core of an influential conception of practical rationality, which has shaped a variety of disciplines to various degrees: theoretical economy, political theory, theoretical historiography, sociology, etc. The application of this conception of rationality in the empirical sciences is based on the assumption that human behaviour is sufficiently rational for social phenomena to be explicable. The fascination it has exerted is, however, due to the way it has been made precise through the formalization of first Ramsey and later Savage.[1]

The plausible idea that rational agents choose their actions to optimize their aims, from now on called the *rational choice paradigm,* is attractive as an instrument of analysis, and also because of the unsatisfactory explanatory power of macro-sociological theories like historical materialism and functionalism.[2] Although the methodological individualism of the social sciences is logically and systematically independent of the rational choice paradigm as an explanatory model, there is a close historical connection between the two. The political use of the superficial contrast between 'critical' macro-sociological theories of historical-materialist extraction and 'right-wing' or market-oriented rational-choice conceptions has been obsolete for a long time. In particular Jon Elster[3] has ensured that ideological controversies no longer mar the discussion. Doubtless, the rational choice-paradigm is booming.

---

1 See Ramsey (1931) and Savage (1954).

2 See Wiesenthal in Elster (1983).

3 See Elster (1979, 1983).

This paradigm has its roots in theoretical economics and statistics, roots which it has not disowned to the present day, and which lead some authors (e. g. G. Becker) to revert to an individualist and egoistic anthropology, which guided economic theory up to the nineteen-thirties. According to this egoistic anthropology, rational agents do not optimize arbitrary personal aims, bet their personal well-being or 'utility'. However, from the perspective of logical empiricism that flourished in this century, a concept like the 'utility' of a person appeared problematic: it did not satisfy the stringent criteria of significance and therefore appeared 'metaphysical'. Thus, the elimination of the classical concept of utility and its replacement by modern utility theory has often been interpreted as a mere conceptual clarification. However, on closer inspection it turns out that this perspective is misleading. The transition to modern utility theory initiated by Ramsey and improved by Savage is at the same time a transition from a conception of practical rationality as instrumental and egoist to a coherence theory of practical rationality. The endeavour to leave microeconomic theory untouched is partly responsible for concealing this fact. The coherence axioms of modern economic theory not only dispense with *egoistical* assumptions (rational agents optimize their personal interests), but are also independent of an *instrumental* conception of practical rationality.

Let $X$ be a set of alternatives which are ordered hierarchically by the preferences of a rational agent. In that case the coherence theory requires that this sequence forms an *ordering relation* $R$ on $X$, i. e. the (weak) preferences of the agent are reflexive, complete and transitive. While *reflexivity* is trivial for (weak) preferences - each alternative is at least as desirable as itself - completeness and transitivity often fail to obtain, as empirical studies have shown.[4] *Completeness* requires of a rational agent that he has a prefence with respect to any of the alternatives $x$, $y$, i. e. he has a (weak) preference for $x$ over $y$, or (inclusive) for $y$ over $x$. *Transitivity* demands that if a rational agent has a weak preference for $x$ over $y$ and for $y$ over $z$, he also has a weak preference for $x$ over $z$. While the condition of reflexivity can be seen as a meaning postulate of the concept 'preference', it seems plausible to view the conditions of completeness and transitivity as genuine postulates of rationality. Accordingly, it is not conceptually excluded that a person may have intransitive or incomplete preferences.

[4] See Tversky/Kahnemann (1984).

However, the aforementioned three ordering conditions do not suffice to pass from the *qualitative* concept of preference to the *quantitative* concept of utility. To do this, one must extend the set of alternatives $X$ probabilistically to $X^*$. The preferences of the agent no longer relate exclusively to the alternatives from $X$, but also to arbitrary probability distributions (lotteries) over $X$. To begin with, the same conditions as before apply to the set $X^*$: the preferences must be reflexive, complete and transitive. In addition, four axioms of coherence must be postulated as follows.

*Reduction:* A rational agent is indifferent between two probability distributions over $X$, if one can be transformed into the other according to the probability calculus.

*Substitution:* If a rational agent is indifferent between a probability distribution $x^*$ and a specific alternative $x$ from $X$, then $x^*$ and $x$ can be substituted in any context without altering the preferences.

*Continuity:* If $x_a$ is the best and $x_z$ the worst alternative in $X$, then for each alternative $x$ from $X$ there is a probability $p$ for $x_a$, such that the rational agent is indifferent between $x$ and the probability distribution $[p\, x_a \,\&\, (1\text{-}p)\, x_z]$.

*Monotony:* Of two probability distributions between $x$ and $y$, the rational agent prefers the one which assigns a higher probability to the better alternative.

None of these axioms refers to specific substantive motives of the agent or makes assumptions about what is of subjective value to the person concerned. The plausibility of these axioms is independent not only of all substantive aims (e. g. of an economic or egoistic kind), but also of whether the rational actions optimize the subjective aims of the agent. There seems to be no logical connection between the instrumentalist egoist theory from which we started and the coherence theory of practical rationality.

It can now be demonstrated that a preference relation $R$ satisfying the above axioms of coherence can be represented by a real-valued function. There is such a function $u$ over $X^*$ which is uniquely determined (it can only vary within the range of positive linear transformation) and for which the following holds:

$$\forall x, y \in X^*: u(x) \geq u(y) \leftrightarrow xRy\,.$$[5]

This so-called utility-theorem is primarily nothing but a harmless representation theorem which transforms the qualitative notion of preference into a quantitative notion, a real-valued function $u$. The possibility of representing preferences by such a function is a necessary and sufficient condition for a given preference relation $R$ satisfying the axioms of coherence. Initially, there is no reason to suspect that this function $u$ is connected with the personal interests of the agent, as traditional economic theory assumes, or, more generally, with his subjective aims (consequentialist interpretation).

We have left completely open what the preferences of the agent are or how they can be empirically determined. The so-called revealed preference-model or rational choice theory identifies actions with the manifest preference for specific elements of $X^*$ in view of the given options. If $X$ is interpreted as a set of states of the world or possible worlds, it is plausible to interpret $u$ over $X$ as representing the subjective evaluation of world-states and $u$ over $X^*|X$ as the expected value, for it can be shown that $u$ is linear in the probabilities, i. e. the following holds: $U(x^*) = p\, u(x) + (1\text{-}p)\, u(x')$, if $x^* = [p\, x \,\&\, (1\text{-}p)\, x']$.

Since the representation theorem can be logically deduced from the axioms which have been stated informally above, anybody who considers the axioms of coherence as an adequate condition for the preferences of a rational agent must, on this interpretation, also recognize that the decisions of a rational agent maximize the utility function $u$ over $X$ (or $X^*$).

The consequentialist interpretation of the utility theorem states that a rational agent evaluates states (this evaluation need not be explicit, it can simply be expressed by the decisions of the agent), and chooses its actions such that the expected value of the (chosen) action which is constituted by the probability distribution of the evaluation of states of the world is maximized. If one makes the additional assumption that this expected value-maximization is the *motive* of a rational agent, the transition from a coherence theory of practical rationality to

[5] See Luce/Raiffa (1957), ch. 2.

a consequentialist theory of optimization is complete. The original theory, according to which a person is rational if her preferences are coherent, has been transformed into a theory according to which an agent is rational if he maximizes the expected value of subjective evaluations of states of the world. That this transition is not logically compelling will be shown in chapter 10 ("Structural Rationality and Coherentism"). There it will be shown that the seeming incompatibility of coherence theory and Kantian rationality can be removed if one reinterpretes the set of alternatives (options). However, with this modification the coherence model can no longer be transformed into the consequentialist optimization model, for in that case it is not states which are optimized; rather, certain features of the action themselves acquire an intrinsic value.

Expanding the application of the rational choice model from the original egoist paradigm of subjectivist consequentialism to the coherence theory involves a fundamental revision of the conception of practical rationality. The consequentialist and coherentist conceptions are logically independent, even if the writings of economists erroneously cite the utility theorem as proof of their equivalence .

## 2. Interactions

Rational choice theory not only deals with situations of risk and uncertainty, but also with situations of interaction. Since this branch of rational choice theory emerged historically from the mathematical analysis of games, it has up to the present day been labelled, misleadingly, as 'game theory'.[6] Game theory and decision theory in the narrow sense investigate individual rational decisions. From this narrow perspective the rational choice is determined relative to a given value function of consequences and the subjective probability function of the circumstances. Of what kind these circumstances are is irrelevant in the first instance. In an interaction situation these circumstances consist in the decisions of other agents (possibly plus additional chance events). For this reason, the expansion of the rational choice-paradigm from the problem of decision theoretic optimization ('playing against nature') to

[6] For a still good introduction see Luce/Raiffa (1957), see also Holler/Illing (1991).

the problem of game-theoretic optimization appears to be unproblematic, at least with regard to interactions in which the decisions of the players are mutually independent (non-cooperative games).

In fact, problems arise with this extension of the rational choice paradigm, since the agent must assume that the other players decide rationally as well, so that mutual expectations concerning the rational decisions of others partly influence the rationality of a decision. In contrast to decision theory in the narrow sense, where the agents' expectations concerning the circumstances are not a subject of the theory, the expectations concerning the decisions of other players now become a subject of the theory insofar as they are based on mutual expectations concerning the rational behaviour of others. For what is rational in a specific interaction situation is itself a subject of game theory. Game theory tries to tackle this problem by establishing only those decisions as rational which are part of the equilibrium points of the interaction.

An equilibrium point is a combination of decisions (or strategies) in which none of the agents involved has an interest in revoking his decision, as long as all the other agents involved stick to their original decisions. One can interpret this assumption as a consequence of the fact that the recommendations of game theory for rational behaviour are potentially public: only those recommendations are admitted which can be made public without thus providing a reason for deviating from the recommendations. With the aid of the concept of common knowledge[7] one can characterize this version of rationality in interaction situations as follows: a decision is rational in an interaction situation if it maximizes the expected value under the assumption of common knowledge. The common knowledge at issue refers to the structure of the interaction situation (1), represented by the mathematical description of the game (in normal or extensive form), the assumption that the parties concerned are rational in the sense of maximizing expected utility (2), and the game-theoretic recommendations for the interaction situation at issue (3). Common knowledge about these three points means: each party knows (1), (2), (3), each party knows that each party knows (1), (2), (3), each party knows that each party knows that each party knows the (1), (2), (3), etc.[8]

---

[7] This notion goes back to Lewis (1969); see also Heal (1978) and Bicchieri (1989).

[8] Lewis (1969) specifies the concept of common knowledge relative to a state of affairs *S* in which every party has reason to believe that *S* indicates to every party

However, the combination of the rational choice paradigm with the assumption of shared knowledge about the aforementioned three propositions leads to problems. Consider e. g. an interaction situation with a single point of equilibrium in mixed strategies, say a 'two by two' game, in which A faces alternatives $a_1$ and $a_2$, B the alternatives $b_1$ and $b_2$, with the following point of equilibrium: there is a 30% probability of A choosing $a_1$, a 70% probability of his choosing $a_2$, and a 60% probability of B choosing $b_1$, and a 40% probability of his choosing $b_2$. The recommendation for rational behaviour hence requires A and B to decide on a probability distribution over $a_1$ and $a_2$ and $b_1$ and $b_2$, respectively (A and B must not choose $a_1$ or $a_2$ and $b_1$ or $b_2$, respectively). The required decision could e. g. be realized by A and B dropping red and white balls into an urn in a mixing ratio respectively of 3 to 7 and 6 to 4, and then realizing their options according to the colour of a ball arbitrarily picked from the urn (the actual decision consists essentially in choosing a particular mixing ratio of balls in the urn). The axiom of continuity presented in section 1 precludes, however, that a rational agent should prefer a probability distribution between two consequences ($a_1$ and $a_2$ or $b_1$ and $b_2$) to both consequences. Independently of the expectations of A and B concerning the decisions of the other person, the decisions for the strategy of an equilibrium cannot, therefore, be recommended as rational according to the ideal of maximizing expected utility.

There is only one expectation which would not render *irrational* choosing the mixed strategy recommended as an equilibrium, namely that the other person opts for the probability distribution over pure strategies determined by the point of equilibrium. But for this special case the choice of any strategy, be it pure ($a_1$ and $a_2$, or $b_1$ and $b_2$, respectively) or mixed (probability distributions over $a_1$ and $a_2$, or $b_1$ and $b_2$, respectively) is equally rational. The common knowledge that the parties are rational does not, therefore, guarantee the expectation that they will opt for the point of equilibrium. Accordingly, the recommen-

---

that every party has reason to believe that $S$ obtains etc. $S$ thus becomes the base of common knowledge. For example, in cases of coordination through mutual agreement this state of affairs is the agreement. In other cases, however, it would be artificial to construct a state of affairs which is the base of common knowledge. Such knowledge often relies on regularities, norms, institutions, which makes it wrong to isolate a particular state of affairs as such a base.

dation 'if there is a single point of equilibrium, then choose the equilibrium strategy' cannot be derived from the concept of optimizing practical rationality.

Moreover, this problem is not confined to a general deficiency of points of equilibrium in mixed strategies, but is exacerbated by specific structures of interaction. Consider e. g. the following interaction structure:

| | | B | |
|---|---|---|---|
| | | $b_1$ | $b_2$ |
| A | $a_1$ | 2/2 | 3/3 |
| | $a_2$ | 3/3 | 1/1 |

With this constellation, because of assuming common knowledge, the parties A and B know that their respective expectations of rationality must lead to the same result because of the symmetric structure of the game. In other words, if $a_1$ is rational for A, $b_1$ must be rational for B and vice versa (the same holds for $a_2$ and $b_2$). If a mixed strategy, i. e. a probability distribution of $a_1$ and $a_2$, is rational for A, with probability $p$ and $a_1$, then a mixed strategy with $p$ for $b_1$ (and (1-$p$) for $b_2$) should be rational for B (and *vice versa*). Usually, the orientation towards an equilibrium in game theory is presented as a consequence of the assumption of common knowledge. Our example shows, however, that the assumption of common knowledge concerning the structure of the game is in conflict with the theory of equilibrium. This can be demonstrated as follows. The two points of equilibrium are $a_2$, $b_1$ and $a_1$, $b_2$. But, due to the symmetry of the interaction situation, neither one of them can be reached without coming into conflict with the assumption of common knowledge concerning the rationality of the interacting parties and the criteria of rationality. The same holds for mixed strategies: for if a mixed strategy with probability $p$ for $a_1$ were an equilibrium strategy for A, the mixed strategy with $p$ for $b_1$ would be an equilibrium strategy for B, because of the symmetry of the interaction situation. However, it is evident that strategies with the same probability for $a_1$ or $b_1$ are not equilibrium strategies for this situation.

For all interaction structures in which the rationality of an individual decision of an agent depends on what decisions are expected by the other parties, who in turn can make at least one of their decisions only dependent on the expectations of their own decisions, problems arise for the combination of optimizing rationality and the assumption of common knowledge. As an example, consider the following interaction structure:

| | | B | |
|---|---|---|---|
| | | $b_1$ | $b_2$ |
| A | $a_1$ | 2/2 | 4/4 |
| | $a_2$ | 3/3 | 1/1 |

If A expects that B will opt for $b_1$, he will opt for $a_2$; if he expects B to opt for $b_2$, A will opt for $a_1$. Equally, for B, $b_2$ is optimal only under the condition that B can expect A to opt for $a_2$. Independently of the expectations about the decisions of the other parties, however, nothing can be said about the rationality of choosing one of these strategies. To put it differently: under the assumption of common knowledge the rational course of action is underdetermined in interaction situations of this kind. In such cases, the same applies to mixed strategies. If A expects that B will opt for the mixed strategy '75% probability for $b_1$ and 25% probability for $b_2$' (0,75 $b_1$ & 0,25 $b_2$), then A is indifferent as between $a_1$ and $a_2$. Both decisions yield the same expected utility, and the same holds for all probability distributions of $a_1$ and $a_2$. If A expects that B will opt for a mixed strategy with a probability for $b_1$ of less than 75%. $a_1$ is optimal for A, while $a_2$ would be so in case of a greater probability for $b_1$. Consequently, even if mixed strategies are included, a recommendation cannot be given on the assumption of common knowledge: rational agents who maximize utility are not in a position to have the expectations which could determine the rationality of their decisions.

The underdetermination of practical rationality emerging from the last example is irritating since the original rational choice paradigm, which has here been extended to situations of interaction, excludes such underdetermination through making practical rationality relative to subjective probabilities and desirabilities.

By contrast, in an interaction situation of the prisoners' dilemma type, rationality, in the sense of the original rational choice paradigm, is strictly determined, but the result is such that doubts about the adequacy of the paradigm arise:

| | | B | |
|---|---|---|---|
| | | $b_1$ | $b_2$ |
| A | $a_1$ | 3/3 | 1/4 |
| | $a_2$ | 4/1 | 2/2 |

In this interaction situation the second option ($a_2$ and $b_2$, respectively) is dominant for both parties: irrespective of the other party's decision, for both parties $a_2$ and $b_2$ are optimal.

If one assumes that a theory of practical rationality has the task of formulating recommendations for action, the questionable character of the rational choice paradigm for prisoners' dilemma style situations is particularly obvious. Imagine A and B seek advice from two decision theorists Tl and T2. Because of the complete symmetry of the situation they can expect that Tl and T2 will give both parties the same advice, i. e. either $a_1$ and $b_1$ or $a_2$ and $b_2$. If T1 recommends $a_1$ and $b_1$ while T2 recommends $a_2$ and $b_2$, it is clear which advice is more adequate: both A and B are better off listening to Tl. However, T2, who is committed to the rational choice paradigm, recommends $a_2$ and $b_2$ as the dominant strategies (and equilibrium); his advice is unsuccessful in situations of this type.

Of course one might object that this apparent failure is merely due to the fact that two types of practice-oriented criteria have been run together: a criterion can guide decisions relative to the preferences of a particular person (individual rationality) or relative to the behaviour of a group (collective rationality). The game-theoretic decision to go for the dominant, non-cooperative decision in prisoners' dilemma situations is individually rational, but collectively irrational, since the state which is reached if both parties interact rationally from an individual point of view is for both worse than a state which would be reached if both adopted the other alternative (the equilibrium in the prisoners' dilemma is not Pareto-optimal).

This defence suffers from two defects, which turn out to be closely related. Firstly, the recommendation of the dominant strategy as part of the single equilibrium of the game cannot be justified by reference to the individualistic character of this recommendation, since the singling out of points of equilibrium in interaction situations is, as we have seen, only legitimate under the assumption of common knowledge, i. e. of a collective component. Accordingly, this kind of justification of non-cooperative strategies in prisoners' dilemma type situations undermines the methodological basis of game theory in general, and forces the rational choice paradigm back to the basic model ('games against nature') discussed in the first section of this chapter. Secondly, even a theory of individual rationality, if it is to be understood normatively and not descriptively, must abide by minimal requirements of universalizability (the problem of the detachability of ought-sentences). It is questionable whether the general recommendation to opt for the non-cooperative strategy in the prisoners' dilemma satisfies these conditions.

Starting in the sixties, empirical investigations have been conducted about the behaviour of people in situations of the prisoners' dilemma type.[9] It emerged that to an astonishing degree people opt for the cooperative alternative, i. e. in an individually non-optimal way, even if they know the structure of the situation and are confronted with a case of one single interaction ('one-shot-PD-game'). The following is a plausible, albeit not the only, interpretation of such cooperative behaviour: An agent cooperates, because she knows that cooperation on both sides is collectively rational. Only under very specific assumptions could it be surmised that altruistic motives play a rôle. (Through the right variation of the payoffs it could even be assertained empirically whether such motives are involved). It is at least intuitively plausible that an agent opts consciously for the cooperative strategy, even if her

[9] See Rapoport/Guyer/Gordon (1976) and Kern/Räder (1988).

subjective evaluations of the four possible results correspond to an interaction of the prisoners' dilemma type. To exclude a *petitio principii*, the prisoners' dilemma must be defined not via the hierarchy of combinations, but exclusively via the consequences of these combinations. In the original story, which underlies the term 'prisoners' dilemma', these consequences are varying prison-terms for each of the parties. The one who does not confess gets, e. g., two years if the other does not confess either, while he gets, say, 12 years if he fails to confess while the other prisoner does confess. The one who confesses is acquitted as a supergrass-witness if the other fails to confess, but gets 10 years if the other confesses as well. Confessing is the non-cooperative strategy here (in what follows abbreviated as '*n*'), failure to confess the cooperative strategy (subsequently '*k*'). The matrix of consequences (prison-terms) looks as follows:

| | | B | |
|---|---|---|---|
| | | $n_2$ | $k_2$ |
| | $n_1$ | 10/10 | 0/12 |
| A | $k_1$ | 12/0 | 2/2 |

We have said that a prisoners' dilemma type of interaction is defined by the subjective preferences over consequences. In this respect, the above interaction situation (with the given consequences in terms of years of imprisonment) is an interaction of the prisoners' dilemma type only if A prefers going free even if this means 10 years longer in prison for B, and if A prefers shortening her prison-term (from 12 to 10 years) even if B's term thereby increases from 0 to 10 years. If $C_A$ are the consequences for A and $C_B$ the corresponding consequences for B, the following relation of preferences defines the interactions of the prisoners' dilemma type:

$$
\begin{array}{ll}
\text{A:} & C_A\,(n,k)/C_B\,(n,k) \\
& C_A\,(k,k)/C_B\,(k,k) \\
& C_A\,(n,n)/C_B\,(n,n) \\
& C_A\,(k,n)/C_B\,(k,n) \\
\text{B:} & C_A\,(k,n)/C_B\,(k,n) \\
& C_A\,(k,k)/C_B\,(k,k) \\
& C_A\,(n,n)/C_B\,(n,n) \\
& C_A\,(n,k)/C_B\,(n,k)
\end{array}
$$

This cumbersome notation was chosen deliberately in order to prevent the choice of representation from including a theoretical prejudice for the revealed preference conception, i. e. the assumption that preferences are revealed in the decisions. If we had confined the representation of preferences for A to the left and for B to the right column, i. e. the consequences for A and B, respectively, this would have implicitly codified the assumption that preferences are exclusively self-oriented.

$$
\begin{array}{lll}
\text{A:} & C_A & (n,k) \\
& & (k,k) \\
& & (n,n) \\
& & (k,n) \\
\text{B:} & C_B & (k,n) \\
& & (k,k) \\
& & (n,n) \\
& & (n,k)
\end{array}
$$

If we had used the sequence of strategic combinations to characterize situations of the prisoners' dilemma type, this would have meant committing ourselves *ab initio* to the conception of rationality which optimizes individual well-being.

| | |
|---|---|
| A: | *n, k* |
| | *k, k* |
| | *n, n* |
| | *k, n* |
| B: | *k, n* |
| | *k, k* |
| | *n, n* |
| | *n, k* |

Let us return to the agent who, knowing the structure of the situation at hand and the C-preferences (i. e. preferences over the consequences of the interaction), opts for the cooperative strategy. Assume that her rationale for this decision is that mutual cooperation is preferable to mutual non-cooperation, which favours a cooperative strategy in cases in which the interaction is symmetrical. Obviously, the preferences of such an agent cannot be presented through the last-mentioned structure of preferences. For, if we assume that all essential information about the four alternatives is given with the corresponding combinations of strategies, this would mean that A goes for *k,k* rather than *n,k* which is contrary to the stated order of preferences. The preferences of such an agent would indeed be inconsistent.

The intention to cooperate can, however, provide a good reason for action. Yet it would be completely erroneous to interpret such cooperative reasons for action as reevaluation of consequences.[10] A rational agent can opt for a cooperative strategy in a prisoners' dilemma even if she prefers the consequences of non-cooperation to those of cooperation for a given decision of the other party. With regard to the given example: a rational agent can refuse to confess even if she prefers going free and 12 years of prison for the other party to 2 years of prison for each, and 10 years of prison for herself and the other to 12 years of prison for herself and going free for the other. Indeed, a person can have cooperative intentions for action only if she does not reevaluate the consequences in such a way that the prisoners' dilemma structure of the interaction situation is altered. In short, the revealed preference orthodoxy logically excludes cooperation as a reason for

---

[10] This interpretation corresponds to the approach based on second-order preferences introduced by Sen (1974) into the discussion of the prisoners' dilemma. I criticize this approach in ch. 8 below.

action, with the result that one must either follow its lead or abandon the revealed preference paradigm in decision theory. Since cooperation undeniably plays an important rôle in our everyday behaviour, and since it cannot be assumed that this behaviour is in general irrational, this provides a strong reason for supposing that the orthodox revealed preference conception is inadequate.

## 3. Collective Agents

The question of the rationality of group decisions (collective decisions) is the subject of an independent branch of decision theory, the logic of collective (or public or social) choice.[11] Independently of the concrete conditions of collective choice (implicit and explicit rules for decision making, institutional frameworks, individual rights, etc.) collective decisions can be presented as an aggregation of individual preferences. For a given set of individual preference relations there is a determinate collective preference relation. In the first instance, the rationality of collective preferences can be assessed in the same way as the rationality of individual preferences: they must be coherent, i. e. satisfy the conditions discussed in section 1. Additionally, the collective preferences must stand in a certain relation to the given individual preferences. At this point, however, problems arise which characterize the logic of collective decisions through a series of impossibility theorems. The best-known of these is Arrow's theorem, which formulates several conditions on the relation between individual and collective preferences which seem indispensable for the latter being rational.[12] One of these is the Pareto-condition, which requires that alternatives which are preferred by all people must also be preferred by the collective. Another condition, that of independence, requires that a

---

[11] The two standard works on the logic of collective decision-making are still Arrow (1951) and Sen (1970). For a survey cf. Sen (1986), Mueller (1979), Rothkirch (1981) and Kern/Nida-Rümelin (1994).

[12] Although the logical analysis of collective decision-making goes back to the eighteenth century (see Condorcet (1785), also Kern/Nida-Rümelin (1994), ch. 3), Arrow's book (1951) marks its real beginning. Ch. 5 of this book develops the so called 'possibility theorem', which is better labelled 'impossibility theorem', since it *prima facie* excludes an aggregation which satisfies reasonable conditions.

collective ordering of two alternatives should not be changed simply by the appearance of a third alternative. Arrow's theorem states that if one allows arbitrary individual preferential relations, restricted only by the coherence conditions of section 1, then the only rule of aggregation which satisfies both the irrelevance and the Pareto-condition is dictatorial, i. e. the collective agent preferences are determined by the preferences of a single person.[13] However, such a rule of aggregation is not just ethically unacceptable, it is also incompatible with the goal of determining collective preferences as plausible aggregates of individual preferences. The second condition of rationality, which requires a reasonable connection between individual and collective preferences, has been violated.

There is an extensive debate about how a satisfactory result can be achieved by weakening one or more of these conditions. The upshot is sobering. Although a dilution of the conditions of coherence of collective preferences from transitivity to mere acyclicity no longer leads to a one-person dictatorship, it still only allows for aggregate functions in which one group has a veto, which amounts to a kind of collective dictatorship ('veto group theorem').[14]

The problematic character of extending the rational choice paradigm to collective agents is brought into particularly sharp relief by the so-called 'Liberal Paradox':[15] the minimal condition on collective rationality, the Pareto-inclusiveness of the aggregate function, conflicts in certain preference structures with the minimal condition of individual freedom of choice. Combining the demand that every individual should have a free choice of at least one alternative with the demand that alternatives which are (weakly) preferred by all individuals are also preferred by the aggregate function can lead to cyclical preferences.

---

[13] On the problem of how to interpret aggregate functions see Nida-Rümelin (1986, 1987a, 1991a) and Tanguiane (1992), who argues for a rehabilitation of dictatorial decision-rules through introducing an element of democratic representation.

[14] Kern/Nida-Rümelin (1994), ch. 4.

[15] The liberal paradox was first discovered by Sen (1970), ch. 6, and has prompted an extensive discussion, the highlights of which are Nozick's (1973, 1974) libertarian proposal to exclude liberal rights from the aggregation, the theorem of Gibbard (1973) and the critique of 'welfarism' by Sen (1979). See Breyer (1978), Krüger/Gärtner (1983), Wriglesworth (1985), Riley (1986), Mezzetti (1987), Barry (1987).

Particularly disconcerting for the rational choice paradigm is the theorem showing the susceptibility of collective decisions to manipulation and strategic voting.[16] The rational choice paradigm starts from individuals who maximize optimal consequences. Consequently, any theory of collective rationality must face up to the question of whether its rules of decision-making are compatible with the possibility that individuals maximize individual utility. The theorem showing how collective decisions are susceptible to manipulation and strategic voting states that individual maximization implies that for any aggregate function individuals have a reason to conceal their preferences. Indeed, there is only one rule of aggregation which is free of strategy, i. e. for which no individual has a reason to feed distorted preferences into the process of aggregation, namely dictatorship. An analogous result emerges for the vulnerability to manipulation of collective decisions. All aggregate functions except for the dictatorial one are vulnerable to manipulation for certain preference structures.

One must not be misled by the fact that the results of the logic of collective decisions are exclusively negative. This does not render the analysis of collective decisions obsolete; on the contrary, it offers a conspicuous analytical tool for explaining the complexity of real collective decisions. But it does undermine the idea that social action results from individually optimizing behaviour in the sense of the original rational choice paradigm, and that collective action constitutes an optimizing collective agent.

## 4. Structural Rationality

The problems confronting the extension of the rational choice paradigm to interaction situations and collective decisions can be seen as *problems of coordination in a wide sense*. Problems of coordination *in a narrow sense* arise in situations in which the different options yield roughly equivalent results, and in which it is a mere matter of coordination which options are chosen. We are dealing with *interpersonal* coordination in a wide sense whenever individual options have to be

[16] See Gibbard (1973), Satterthwaite (1975), Schmeidler/Sonnenschein (1978).

coordinated. Intrapersonal coordination, by contrast, is coordination of the options of a single person.

Just as in the prisoners' dilemma individual maximization leads to a situation in which all parties are worse off than otherwise, leading a good life intrapersonally depends on the agent not acting in an optimizing way in each single situation, but subjecting herself to restraints which only provide structure and coherence to her life.[17] The idea that the required minimum of collective rationality could be ensured exclusively through sanctions is certainly misguided. At least, this way of harmonizing optimizing rationality and collective rationality (it might be labelled the 'Hobbesian programme') has only a very restricted application to everyday interactions. In addition to sanctions, there is no doubt that virtues (acquired behavioural dispositions in modern parlance) play an important rôle in ameliorating the problem of coordinating individual maximization. In game-theoretic terms, sanctions of structurally rational behaviour constitute a change in the pay-offs, while dispositions restrict the class of available strategies. The numerous empirical phenomena of self-imposition indicate that people impose sanctions upon themselses (more or less consciously) to exclude options which are pernicious overall, i. e. from the perspective of intrapersonal coordination even if they are optimal in the short term.

In addition to social or legal sanctions (sanctions through custom or legislation), dispositional conditioning and acts of self-imposition, there is also the empirical phenomenon of intentional rule-following: there are situations in which a rational agent follows a rule, although she knows she need not fear sanctions for violating that rule, and although her dispositions have not been moulded in the direction of abiding by the rule. Such rule-following is intentional if decisions are made with the intention of following the rule in question. Talking about 'rules' may encourage the misunderstanding that one is dealing with rules which are explicit, which have been codified, or which are established through morality. 'Rule' is here used in a catholic sense. Thus it

---

[17] Slote (1989) develops an interesting attack - ultimately inspired by a puritanical attitude - on conceptions of rationality based on optimization. Aporetic consequences of optimizing rationality are illustrated with reference to sociological and biological facts by Elster (1979, 1983, 1986); see also Campbell/Sowden (1985) and the interesting conception of 'bounded rationality' in Simon (1983a).

would be a case of rule-following to adopt the collectively rational option in certain variations of the prisoners' dilemma. Since inter- and intrapersonal coordination is a matter of choosing an option which fits into a desirable structure of actions or strategies, this might also be called *structural rationality*. The fact that invoking e. g. a morally approved rule provides a good reason to choose an act which conforms to the rule shows that talking about 'rationality' makes sense here: an action is rational if there is a good reason for performing it. Structural rationality is also involved if an agent decides to feed her actual preferences into a process of aggregation, in spite of knowing that only a distorted representation of these preferences would maximize her preferences.

Coordination provides a good reason for action: it demands that particular actions at a specific time are fitted into an approved structure of individual or social activity. The identification of practical rationality with (pointwise) optimization of consequences, on the other hand, allows only two explanatory models for the phenomenon of coordinative and cooperative action: the Leviathan-model, and the model of dispositional conditioning (*homo sociologicus*). The Leviathan-model explains coordinative behaviour by reference to manifest or concealed sanctions (in the case of sanctions *in foro interno* one might talk of the Freud-model). The model of dispositional conditioning explains such behaviour by reference to acquired dispositions which restrict the freedom of action of the agent (in sociological parlance this comes out as rôle-models). The gap which is left even by a skilful combination of the two models reveals a deficiency in the theory of practical rationality: even behaviour which is genuinely coordinative can be rational. The motive to act in a certain way because this fits into a desired structure of social or individual action can be rational, the action well-justified, namely structurally rational. Such structural rationality is compatible with the coherence-version of the rational choice-paradigm, but not with the consequentialist interpretation of that paradigm.

## 5. Rational Choice and Ethics

The idea of rationality as optimizing consequences carries over into ethical theory if one assumes that a moral action should be rational. Of course there is the possibility of restricting the application of the rational choice-paradigm, notably by applying it only to what Kantians call pragmatic and technical imperatives, while moral imperatives are subject to other criteria, e. g. that of universalizability.[18] However, it is more plausible to harmonize rational and ethical considerations through a suitable modification of the value function that is to be optimized. Moral and egoistic behaviour would then be distinguished not by the question of consequentialist optimization, but by the content of the value function. Rational moral behaviour, in contrast to rational but non-moral behaviour, would maximize an impartial, in the limiting case invariant, value function. Harsanyi has pursued this approach with particular stringency.[19] Because this approach extends Bayesian rationality into ethics, it might be labelled 'Ethical Bayesianism'.

To identify the morally correct with the optimization of a common value function is intuitively appealing: in this way the consequentialist conception of rationality can be retained, while the substantial moral questions are referred to the discussion of the appropriate values. In fact, however, closer consideration shows that problems of coordination and cooperation arise even if one makes the weighty assumption of shared value functions, and become even more acute if these functions vary between different people.[20]

---

[18] This is suggested by Suppes (1973) and criticized in Nida-Rümelin (1987a), §10.
[19] Since the early fifties Harsanyi has developed different versions of this pure rational ethics in a series of articles (1953, 1955, 1958, 1976, 1977a, 1977b, 1978, 1979, 1980, 1985).
[20] Cf. ch. 7.

CHAPTER 3

# Actions and Intentions

## 1. Intentionality

Intentionality[1] is the property of mental states through which they are directed to (or are about) objects or states of affairs in the world.[2] 'Intentionality' and 'Intensionality' are closely related. In 'intensional contexts' coextensional predicates cannot be substituted *salva veritate* under all circumstances. When we describe intentions, we generally have to deal with intensional contexts.[3] Relying closely on Brentano, R. Chisholm[4] has developed a conception of linguistically characterized intentionality which transfers the originally metapsychological question into a question asking for the logical form of sentences describing psychological phenomena. In this way, the close interrelation between intentionality and intensionality is demonstrated.

Convictions are convictions about something being the case, fears are fears that something is going to happen, wishes are wishes to do something, to have something, to experience something, suppositions are suppositions that something will be or has been the case etc. Intentionality is a typical feature of many but not of all mental states: it

---

[1] Chisholm asks how objective reference - resp. intentionality - is possible. How is it possible to direct ones thoughts towards an object? In order to answer this question he develops a Platonist ontology assuming the existence of eternal viz. *abstract* objects: *There are* properties, relations and states of affairs. Here it is not necessary to clarify whether this procedure is necessary and appropriate. Therefore we will leave aside these ontological questions in the following which, however, requires the reader to translate the ontological wording ('An action is...', 'there are intentions which...' etc.) in doubtful cases into a language using the term 'states of affairs' ('it is the case that the person acts intentionally...'). See Chisholm (1981), esp. ch. 2 and 4.

[2] See Anscombe (1965), also Searle (1983), ch. 1.

[3] This connection, however, does not justify the claim that intensionality is a special form of intentionality. See Kneale (1968) and Prior (1969).

[4] Drawing upon Frege, Chisholm uses the term 'indirect reference' for referential opacity, see Chisholm (1972).

is useful to start off from a narrow notion of intentionality not ascribing to every 'being conscious' a 'being conscious of something'. When I am conscious of happiness, the happiness is not necessarily a happiness about something.[5] With this narrow conception of intentionality the identification of 'consciousness' and 'intentionality' is ruled out. Wishes, for example, are necessarily intentional, but not always conscious - *vice versa* I can be conscious of my (non-intentional) dejection. Although intentionality is not genuinely linguistical[6] - it is meaningful to say that the lurking cat in front of the hole *believes*[7] that there is a mouse inside - there is, as Searle has convincingly demonstrated, an interesting parallel between the representation of states of affairs by intentional states and the representation of states of affairs by speech acts.[8]

Speach act theory[9] distinguishes propositional content from the illocutionary rôle in which the former is presented. Analogously, one can distinguish the propositional content of intentional states from the

---

5 See for this point Searle's treatment of self-referential forms of intentionality, Searle (1983), ch. 2 and 3.

6 An important movement in the philosophy of language derives language logically from intentionality, whereas a widespread interpretation of Wittgenstein's later philosophy assumes the opposite relation between language and intentionality. Essential for this movement are H. P. Grice's papers 'Meaning' (Grice 1957) and 'Utterer's Meaning and Intentions' (Grice 1969), see also Bennett (1973) and Lewis (1969, 1975).

7 Only when we ascribe intentionality to higher animals, statements such as 'the restless behaviour of the dog is *understandable,* since he *expects* the family to come home when hearing the familiar sounds of the engine' etc. become meaningful. See Spaemann (1978), p. 481: 'The scientific attempt to interpret the dog's walking to the feeding bowl without the word 'hunger' and its barking upon the return of his master without the word 'joy' alway has something phantastic.' (my translation).

8 Searle (1983).

9 J. L. Austin has developed speach act theory with the aim of clarifying the usage of linguistic terms. This is arrived at by asking for the actions which are performed by a speaker when making a certain utterance. John, who says to a visitor of his town that 'There is a bull', performes in the first place the locutionary act of saying that there is a bull. At the same time, however, he is warning the visitor - Austin calls this the illocutionary act. And perhaps John frightens the visitor with his utterance - this Austin calls the perlocutionary act. Austin's approach was further developed by John Searle and is meanwhile widely applied not only in the philosophy of language but also in linguistics, sociology and psychology. See Austin (1962), Searle (1969) and Wunderlich (1976). A good critical introduction to speech act theory is Savigny (1974), ch. 3 and Stegmüller (1979a), ch. 1, § 3.

*attitude* with which it is presented. An example for a speech act is: 'I warn you of this event.' The propositional content of this speech act is that the event will occur; the speech act is the warning. An example for an intentional state is: 'I hope that the sun will shine tomorrow.' The propositional content is that the sun will shine tomorrow, the attitute is hope.

In the same way as there are speech acts without propositional content,[10] there are intentional states without propositional content. All intentional contents are characterized by certain attitudes, but one cannot talk of *propositional* attitudes since not all intentional states have a (full-blown) propositional content. The propositional content of 'John loves beefsteak' may be 'John is eating beefsteak', but also 'John loves Mary' characterizes an intentional state although it is difficult if not impossible to state the propositional content in the latter case.

To several, namely the *assertive* speach acts (claiming, supposing, etc.), predicates such as 'true' or 'false' can be applied. Analogously, we can say of assertive intentional states that they are correct or true resp. false: there are, for example, correct suppositions. Others, the *directive* speach acts such as requests or commands, cannot be true or false, but they can be fulfilled if there is a change with respect to what would have happened[11] if the addressed person had not acted according to the request or command. They are corresponding to directive intentional states such as hopes, wishes and intentions. Such as the single speech act of commanding is not true or false, the singular derective intentional state of wishing is not true or false but it is fulfilled or not. There are also intentional states corresponding to the commissive type of speech acts (e. g. promises), such as feeling obliged, being loyal etc. The closer interrelation between commissive speech acts and commissive intentional states often becomes apparent in wordings of the form '*x* feels *y*': 'I feel obliged', 'I feel requested', etc. The distinction between assertive, directive and commissive intentional states is - as it is with speech acts - not a complete disjunction: while one can subsume 'love' (under certain circumstances) under the directive intentional states

---

[10] See for this point E. v. Savigny's critique of the Austinian distinction between locutionary and illocutionary acts, Savigny (1974), pp. 158 ff.

[11] This points towards the *counterfactual* element implicit in all agency, see v. Wright (1977) and (1977-81).

(love can remain unfulfilled), this is not the case with 'surprise' or 'being happy', although both states surely are not assertoric or commissive.

For our purposes the most interesting connection between speech acts and intentional states concerns speech acts and intentional states with propositional content. Numerous speech acts with propositional content are subject to a *condition of sincerity* without necessarily failing when it is not fulfilled: I can recommend something without being convinced about the quality of the recommended, but this recommendation would not be sincere. Something similar is true of the *assertive* speech acts of claiming, denying, describing etc.: *directive* speech acts (as e. g. commanding; it is not a sincere command if I do not want the addressee to obey the command) and *commissive* speech acts (as promises; it is not a sincere promise if I do not intend to keep it). When the condition of sincerity is fulfilled, it is possible to infer from a singular speech act to a singular mental state.[12] If the recommendation (speech act) which my neighbour gave me was sincere, then he has certain beliefs (intentional states) about the quality of the recommended. If his promise (speech act) was sincere then he intends (intentional state) to perform the action (or: one of the actions in the case of more than one alternative) which keeps the promise.

The condition of sincerity, however, is not only a contingent condition which - if it is fulfilled - connects speech act and intentional state. There is, furthermore, a special relation between speech act and intentional state which can be regarded as a kind of 'representation'. This can be seen from utterances which combine a speech act with the negation of the corresponding intentional state and which, therefore, are contradictory or, perhaps more appropriate, *self-defeating*.

Examples:
a) *assertive*: 'I claim that Columbus was Spanish but I am not sure whether Columbus was Spanish.'

---

[12] See Searle (1982). Searle distinguishes two types of speech acts with propositional content, 'representatives' and 'directives'. Representatives carry a condition of truthfulness with them while directives typically are followed by attempts of the addressee to influence the actual world to the extent that the respective proposition is fulfilled. See also the theory of J. Bennett on the (basically) non-linguistic basis of concepts of meaning and intention, Bennett (1976).

b) *commissive*: 'I promise to come tomorrow but I do not intend to come tomorrow.'
c) *directive*: 'I command you to leave but I do not wish you to leave.

In all of these three cases the intentional state does not follow logically from the speech act in the sense that

a) '*x* claims *y*' implies '*x* is sure that *y*';
b) '*x* promises *y*' implies '*x* intends *y*';
c) '*x* commands *y*' implies '*x* wishes *y*'.

Nevertheless the belief that the speaker does not have the corresponding intentional state 'destroys' the speech act: it cannot be performed in this combination. While infelicities of type 'Gamma 1' in Austins sense do not render the coming about of the speech act impossible,[13] the mere becoming known - in most cases the mere publicity of the speaker not being upright - causes (as the examples given show) in fact a failure of the speech act. A command of which the addressee knows that it is not meant seriously is generally not obeyed. In a certain sense one can even say that the command was not given, since 'the addressee knew that it was not meant serious'. The convention of commands, however, requires that the one giving the command wishes compliance. In another sense, one can say that the command was 'formally' given. This, however, also is typical for other cases of failures in the case of explicitely performative utterances.[14] When John says with a happy voice and a mocking face: 'I warn you, over there is a bull', then he has warned the visitor 'formally' but not 'really'. It would be inappropriate to claim in this case that he has warned the visitor in the illocutionary but not the perlocutionary sense since the visitor *could* not take the warning serious under these circumstances - and insofar it was not a warning in the illocutionary sense. This feature of natural language suggests that the interpretation of an intentional state as something which is *represented* by the corresponding speech act is correct.

To avoid possible confusion it is necessary to point out that this concept of representation is different from the one used by Searle for

---

[13] See Austin's (1962) fourth lecture.
[14] See Austin's sixth lecture.

the relation between speech acts and propositional content.[15] For Searle, each speech act consists of a representation of generally non-mental states of affairs and objects. The *statement* that it is raining represents the same state of affairs as the *hope* that it rains. The command directed to John to leave the room represents a certain action of John and not the intentional state of the commander. This concept of representation, however, is already covered by the notion of 'propositional content'. Furthermore, speech acts represent (in the meaning used here) in a quite straightforward sense mental states as the examples above have shown. Many speech acts have a propositional content, some are directed towards objects, events or states of affairs - but the representation of something non-linguistical through something linguistical is also present in the speech act/mental state-relation. This relation seems to be universal: each speech act represents a mental state, in many cases (and these are those which are interesting for our present concern) an *intentional mental state*.

A warning or a command can be obeyed, a promise can remain unkept, an assertion can be correct: not all but many speech acts have *conditions of fulfilment*. If a speech act has conditions of fulfilment, then the intentional state represented in the speech act also has conditions of fulfilment, and both these conditions are identical. An assertion (singular speech act) is true if and only if it is true that the conviction (intentional state) represented in the assertion is correct. A promise (speech act) is fulfilled/kept if and only if the plan (intentional state) represented in the promise is executed. The command is obeyed if and only if the wish represented in the command has come true. Intentions to act characterize a special kind of intentionality. An intention to act is a special intentional mental state closely related to actions. Generally, an action is the condition for the fulfilment of an intention. However, one has to distinguish between different kinds of intentionality with regard to actions. Only for one type of intentions it is true that an action is the condition for the fulfilment of the corresponding intention.

---

[15] See Searle (1983), ch. 1, sec. II.

## 2. Actions as Intentional Behaviour

The intentionality of an action is part of the concept of action. An 'unintentional action' is an empty concept. With regard to unintentional behaviour one can answer, e. g., the question 'What have you done there?' by 'Oh, I have thrown down the vase', but when I ask myself what I have done wrong, which of my actions in the last half hour were wrong, then I will not come to the conclusion that throwing down the vase was a wrong action, even if I regret this happening (possibly it was wrong to step so close to the vase with all these other people around). If I have not thrown down the vase unintentionally, then I have thrown it down *intentionally*$_0$ - it is only in this case that this happening corresponds to a (probably blameworthy) action.

Another example: somebody is drunk-driving and hitting another person with his car, and the injured dies later on in hospital. What has the driver done? He has killed a man. Surely, this killing was unintentional. Was it an action? Here as well it is striking that the driver will, when considering which of his actions in the last half hour were wrong, not come to the conclusion that it was wrong to kill the other. Presumably he has done many things wrong in the last half hour: perhaps he has had an intensive conversation with his companion in the car or he has drunken two glasses more than he could stand. However, the killing itself is not part of the class of wrong actions. The killing was not an action of the driver. Obviously, one can *blame* a person for certain elements of action in the behaviour: the driver is accused of certain aspects of his behaviour only insofar as these aspects correspond to his actions.

This fact constitutes the starting point for H. L. A. Hart's proposal to relate the concept of action closely to the notion of responsibility.[16] This proposal, however, which is supported by legal practise and developed with an intention stemming from legal philosophy is not of help for a restriction of the notion of action, since the concept of responsibility is too unprecise. So the driver is, in a certain sense, responsible for the death of the other, he has a corresponding emotion of guilt, his insurance will be liable for the survivor's pension etc. but on the other hand he will not be sentenced for having committed murder or manslaughter but rather for involuntary manslaughter. Only if ac-

---

[16] Hart (1948/49), see also Pitcher (1960) and Feinberg (1970).

tions are involved, there is personal responsibility, but the relation '*x* is responsible for *y*' admits for *y* more than only actions performed by *x* but also (among other things) certain - not all - consequences of an action of *x*.

A final example: when an experienced driver changes gears he is doing that generally not unintentionally - unintentionally the change happens when he, say, wants to adjust the mirror and in the course of doing this touches the gear shift. Nevertheless there need not be an intention *preceeding* the action of gear-changing (at a certain trigger level of the noise of the engine he normally changes gears). He also could have refrained from changing gears, but one then cannot say in the same way that he could have refrained from gear changing when adjusting the mirror. Insofar the changing of gears in the first case is a controlled, conscious and intentional$_O$ happening, whereas in the second case it is an uncontrolled, unconscious and unintentional happening. This difference can also be brought out by saying 'he intentionally changed gears' in one case and 'he changed gears without intention' in the other.

On could be tempted to interpret the occurences or results connected to the actions as conditions for the fulfilment of intentions$_O$. However, this attempt fails facing examples of the following kind: suppose, the condition for the fulfillment of the intention$_O$ which is part of the action 'changing gears intentionally' is the process of gear shift itself. Then this intention would be fulfilled if some device accidentially causes the shift at the same time. There are two options to avoid this kind of paradoxical consequences:

1) Complex causal happenings are assumed as conditions of fulfilment of an intention$_O$, such that not only the process of changing gears as such but also the causal conditions of its coming about are constituents of the conditions of fulfilment of the corresponding intention$_O$.

2) One accepts talking about intentions$_O$ only as a version of talking about 'doing things intentionally', while '*i* did *x* intentionally' does not imply that *i* had an intention in the usual sense; intentions have as intentional states (propositional) conditions of fulfilment while this is not true of intentions$_O$.

The fist attempt to solve the problem cannot be right since for every condition of fulfilment it seems possible to construct a process which *causally* brings about theses conditions without there being an intentional action corresponding to this process. Another argument for the second solution is that although linguistically one can for '$i$ did $x$ intentionally' also say '$i$ did $x$ with an intention', one cannot find a reasonable answer to the question 'what intention did he have?' in these cases, or that reasonable answers refer to intentions of another type, namely either to intentions which precede an action or to motivating intentions.

## 3. Three Types of Intentions

Something can be done or realized intentionally$_o$ without a *preceding* intention, as in the example of changing the gears in the car: not every action has a preceding intention. Actions without preceding intentions are characterized by the fact that the agent, before acting, knew what he was going to do. Actions without preceding intentions are realized without the agent already knowing before that he was going to perform the respective action.

If Bill intends to kill Carillo, this intention will be fulfilled if Bill kills Carillo. However, it will not be fulfilled if Carillo dies in another way, e. g. by a falling rock. Furthermore, the intention of Bill will not even then be fulfilled if Bill unintentionally kills Carillo.[17] The basic condition for the fulfillment of a preceding intention is not just some happening or event, but an intentional$_o$ action. Intentions of this type do not form a 'conceptual' element of an action.[18]

---

[17] Cf. Chisholm (1966).

[18] Intentions$_v$ must therefore also be taken into consideration as causal determinants of actions. To this type of intentions the objection made to action-theoretic causalism - that intentions cannot be regarded as causes for actions because they are logically connected with actions - cannot be applied. A very pointed elaboration of this argument can be found in Melden (1961), esp. ch. 11 and 12. Further important critics of causalism, whose argumentation is also primarily based on the argument of the so-called logical connection, are Anscombe (1957), Foot (1962), Kenny (1963), Taylor (1964), Bennett (1965), Taylor (1966), Stoutland (1970). A systematic critical discussion of anticausalistic arguments can be found

Formulations like 'he did *y* with the intention *x*' refer to a third type of intentions which we call *motivating intentions*. Intentions of this type motivate a respective action, although the action itself is not the condition for the fulfillment of the intention. *A fortiori* a motivating intention is not an element of the action itself. In many cases, however, the conditions for the fulfillment of motivating intentions are *other*, different actions - therefore the conditions for the fulfillment of a person's motivating intentions are in any case causally or conceptually closely connected with the actions of this person.

If I give somebody a medicine with the motivating intention that he recovers, the condition for the fulfillment of this intention is a possible and desired consequence of my action, but not the action itself. Put more precisely, however, this example also shows the closeness of the intention to the action: the motivating intention I have is to *contribute* with my action to the recovery of the person. Therefore, the intention does not have the proposition 'that he may not be ill (any longer)' as its object, but the contribution of the agent to the person's recovery (as the condition for the fulfillment of the intention). Consequently, we have to distinguish:

1) *Intentions*$_o$ as elements of the respective actions. Intentions$_o$ we also call *action-inherent intentions*.
2) *Intentions*$_v$ as *intentions which precede* an action. These intentions are not action-inherent: the same action may also be realized without this preceding intention. The condition for the fulfillment of preceding intentions are intended$_o$ actions.
3) *Motivating intentions*$_m$ which are neither constitutive elements of actions and which nor have actions as the condition for their fulfillment.

A preceding intention$_v$ does not motivate the realization of an action which is the condition for the fulfillment of this preceding intention. It may motivate other actions, e. g. actions which have as their consequence another action which then is the condition for the fulfillment of the intention$_v$. A preceding intention rather has the character of a decision. 'I have the intention to do *x*' means - according to the situation -

in Beckermann (1977). Interesting arguments for a causalistic conception are provided by Gean (1965/66).

more or less the same as 'I have decided to do *x*, given that I will not be hindered to do it by circumstances I do not know yet.' Preceding intentions can neither be referred to as motivations or as reasons for a respective[19] action, because their close relationship to decisions implies that the need to give reasons for an action is transferred to the intentions which are fulfilled by this action.

Intentions$_m$, on the other hand, can always be referred to as reasons for actions (and their intentions$_v$). Intentions$_m$ for an action $H$ often are intentions$_v$ for another action $H'$, in which $H'$ is the consequence (not the result) of action $H$. With logical necessity this series of actions leads to a concluding action $H_z$, and the reason for $H_z$ can only be such intentions$_m$ which are not preceding intentions for any (other) action.[20]

An example may serve to illustrate these conceptual differentiations: A nurse (*S*) sits next to the bed of a patient (*P*), gets up, goes over to the medicine cabinet, takes out a bottle, goes back to *P*, gives him the medicine, sits down beside his bed again, waits a little while, gets up again, goes over to the wash-basin, prepares cold compresses, etc. One can easily imagine a whole series of procedures, activities and actions which go on for a couple of days: 'The nurse took care of the patient.' This procedure, continuing for days, includes a series of intentional$_o$ actions. But apart from that, *S* now and then also does something unintentionally$_o$ - not concerning her specific actions, but concerning her general behaviour. Only a part of the intentional$_o$ actions, which together with unintentional$_o$ activities form the complex

[19] 'Respective' here replaces the awkward formulation 'for an action which is the condition for the fulfillment of the preceding intention', or more correctly: 'for the action in question which is one of those actions that are the condition for the fulfillment of the preceding intention'.

[20] The reason for a concluding action does of course not necessarily have to be an intention$_m$, other intentional states, even without any propositional content, can be reasons for an action as well. Yet we first want to concentrate on the rôle of intentions, because according to the consequentialist conception this specific type of intentional states is particularly closely connected with rationality of action: for a rational person it is typical to act according to intentions, not just on the base of momentary feelings, states of mind, etc. The fact that the agent is conscious of his 'intentions' even seems to be analytically true, whereas most of all other intentional attitudes which can be action determinants do not have to be 'intentional' in the sense that the agent is conscious of them.

procedure of nursing, are conditions for the fulfillment of preceding intentions$_v$. When *S* moves the spoon in a certain way in order not to spill the medicine, there is no corresponding preceding intention for doing so: *S* is so much acquainted with this kind of action that she does not need any preceding intention in order to move the spoon in the correct way. The intention$_v$ restricts itself to giving *P* the medicine and is fulfilled by giving it to him. The specific realization of this action is intentional$_o$, but it does not follow a preceding intention$_v$. *S* got up in order to go over to the medicine cabinet. This getting up certainly is an action. It was not realized unintentionally, therefore it was an intentional$_o$ action. This action was realized, because *S* wanted to take out the medicine from the cabinet: *S* had the intention to take out the medicine - *S* got up with the intention to take out the medicine. Probably *S* did not for the first thing have the intention to get up and then fulfilled this intention by getting up. On the contrary, rather, there did not exist any preceding intention for this action. For the action of getting up, the intention to take out the medicine is only the motivating, not a preceding intention. The condition for the fulfillment of this intention is the relatively complex intentional action to take out the medicine.

Over the entire activity of nursing expands a multistratified fine-meshed network of preceding and motivating intentions. The more experienced the nurse is, the bigger the meshs of the network will be (because an increasing part of the entire activity will be performed without preceding intentions, even if, in general, still performed intentionally$_o$), and the network will do with less stratifications. More complex activities turn into basic activities - in other words: the part of those actions which are not composed of several other actions will increase. The entire activity of nursing is certainly intentional (*S* does not take care for *P* just by accident or unintentionally), and in this respect we can - even if it seems slightly artificial - regard this entire activity as one complex action. This entire activity or complex action is led by the intention to contribute to *P*'s recovery. And it is this intention which structures the whole network of all other possible intentions concerned. With regard to this superordinate intention all other remaining intentions, preceding or motivating, have the function of mere means. Obviously, there is no action which is the condition for the fulfillment of the superordinate intention$_m$, if we do not want to regard 'to-contribute-to-*P*'s-recovery' itself as an action. To the superordinate intention corresponds the superordinate wish that *P* may recover. Only by this corresponding wish the network of intentions which structures the entire activity is definitely connected with the outside world; because the condition for the fulfillment of this intentional state is a natural proposition, whereas the conditions for the fulfillment of intentions are never independent from actions. *S* can *wish*, but she cannot *intend* the recovery of *P*. If *S* knows that she herself cannot contribute to the recovery of *P*, then it does not make any sense, if *S* says that she intends to get *P* recovered. But *S* can wish that *P* may recover, even if she might not be able to contribute to it. But if *S* wishes that *P* may recover, and if she has the possibility to contribute to it (by certain actions), and if she knows this, then *S* has a respective superordinate (motivating) intention, from which the whole network of motivating and preceding intentions which will guide her (nursing) activity develops.[21]

[21] The concept of a practical syllogism, going back to Aristotle (*Nicomachean Ethics* 1146ff.) and further developed particularly by G. H. v. Wright, which says that we can infer an action of a person from the person's wish to realize this action (a conative premise), and an empirical condition she knows of, can be reconstructed as a logical connection between intentions - cf. Nida-Rümelin (1990).

CHAPTER 4

# Bayesian Consequentialism and Consequential Reasons for Action

## 1. The Bayesian Criterion

A decision is *decision-theoretically reconstructable*, if it is rational according to the Bayesian criterion: A decision is rational if it maximizes the (subjective) expected value of the (subjective) utility of the agent.

In order to assess this criterion we will examine two theories of rational decision which will be called T1 and T2. As a heuristic means we introduce the concept of an '*(ideally) rational person regarding theory T*': the decisions made by the (ideal) rational person regarding T fulfill the conditions of rational decision required by T. In every situation, the rational person regarding T can choose from a definite set of decision alternatives (T1a). Additionally, she has a (well-defined) utility function, i. e. to every event (state or course of the world) she can assign a real number as the (cardinal) degree of her (subjective) preferences and valuations (T1b). And finally she has, at any point in time, a coherent (subjective) allocation of probabilities over all sets of future events (states or courses of the world) (T1c). At any time the rational person regarding T1 maximizes the subjective expected value of her subjective valuation function (Bayesian criterion).

T1 requires a lot of a rational person. A consistent valuation of events must take into account their causal connections as well. The rational person must, therefore, in her valuation also be able to consider entire chains of events or courses of the world, and, particularly, she must be able to assess the consequences of her decisions not just with regard to the present state, but also with regard to future events and developments - even if still far ahead. At least she must be able to assign consistent probabilities to all possible courses of the world connected with every action: to a rational person, T1 assigns a coherent allocation of probabilities over the set of all logically possible courses of the world. Moreover, the rational person regarding T1 must be able to sum up the different criteria and aspects which influence her decision in one single numerical valuation. This, however, includes the comparative assessment of entities which are difficult to be compared with each other: e. g. the personal welfare on the one hand, and the standard of distributive justice on the other.

It is quite obvious that the application of T1 has some difficulties, both as an action-guiding normative theory and as an analytical instrument for the 'rational reconstruction' of human decision behaviour.[1] Possibly, the ideal rational person regarding T1 is fictitious and does not offer any orientation for real actions. Accordingly, the attempt to reconstruct decisions of actual persons with regard to T1 could fail, because there are no or too little correspondences between actual persons and the ideal rational person regarding T1. But even if this is the case, it does not exclude that T1 still defines the ideal type of rational decision. There are different philosophical opinions about the question whether such an abstract model still makes sense. The successes achieved in the theoretical natural sciences, however, show that there is a great methodological tolerance in the application of ideal type abstractions. With the critique that the Bayesian model lacks applicability, nothing is said about the question as to whether Bayesian consequentialism could not still be an adequate ideal type characterization of rational decision. The second theory of rational decision T2 we have already come across in chap. 2, sec. 1. It does not offer a *criterion* for the choice of a rational decision but formulates some minimal conditions the preferences of a rational person should satisfy. These conditions can be understood as elements of a theory of practical coherence. If the preferences of a person fulfill these conditions of T2 then there is a real-valued function over the range of objects to which the preferences are directed. If these objects are collected within the set $A$, then the following three properties of this value function $u$ hold:

1) $\forall a,a' \in A:[a \geq a' \leftrightarrow u(a) \geq u(a')]$.

---

[1] H. Simon even goes so far to conclude: 'Conceptually, the SEU [= subjective expected utility] model is a beautiful object deserving a prominent place in Plato's heaven of ideas. But vast difficulties make it impossible to employ it in any literal way in making actual human decisions', Simon (1983b).

2) The function $u$ is linear, i. e.

$$\forall a, a' \in A : \exists p, 0 \leq p \leq 1 : \left[ u(\langle p/a \& (1-p)/a' \rangle) = pu(a) + (1-p)u(a') \right]$$

3) Such a function is, positive linear transformations excepted, definitely and unambiguously defined by the preferences of the respective person. This means: if $u$ and $u'$ are two functions which both satisfy (1), then the following holds:

$$\exists r \in IR^{+} \; \exists s \in IR : \forall a \in A : \left[ u'(a) = ru(a) + s \right].$$

In the economic literature this kind of function $u$ is usually called 'utility function'. Whether this term is adequate or rather mistaken depends on the 'character' of the preferences which underlie this function. In case they express moral convictions, the term would certainly be misleading. The fact that preferences can be represented by a function $u$ with the features listed above only gives evidence for their coherence with regard to probabilistic alternatives, but it does not say anything about their motives (their content).

The theorem has the character of a *metrification-theorem*: it asserts that under certain conditions on the basis of a comparative concept of weak preferences a quantitative valuation function can be defined definitely and unambigously (linear transformation excepted). Everybody who considers the above mentioned conditions of T2 to be the minimal conditions for ideally rational behaviour is for logical reasons compelled to accept that in her decision behaviour the rational person maximizes the valuation function $u$.[2]

If the function $u$ of the theorem was identical with the subjective valuation function of (T1b), and if it corresponded to the set of the subjective probability distributions of (T1c), the theories of rational decision T1 and T2 would be logically equivalent. But an equivalence of T1 and T2 would also mean: everybody considering the postulates of T2 to be sensible conditions for rational behaviour must accept con-

[2] A proof in which the terminology we have introduced here is used can be found in Kern/Nida-Rümelin, (1994), ch. 2.

sequentialism in the form of T1, i. e. the 'Bayesian version of consequentialism'.

In order to decide whether T1 and T2 are really equivalent, it is necessary to examine the interpretation of the basic terms employed in them. In T1 we spoke of a rational person's subjective valuations of events. But it has not been said anything in T1 about the definition corresponding to this valuation. In general the utility theorem is interpreted as a possibility of such a definition. This, however, would already presuppose the equivalence of T1 and T2 - and is therefore of no use for us.

## 2. Consequential Reasons for Actions

Let us suppose the following statement to be true:
'Person *P* has a reason for *h*', i. e. more exactly: '*P* has, at time *t*, a reason to perform action *h*': *G*(*P*, *t*, *h*).

1) Does it follow from *G*(*P*, *t*, *h*) that there exists something (a goal *z*) which *P* wants to attain by realizing *h*?
2) Does it follow from *G*(*P*, *t*, *h*) that *P* knows *G*?
3) Does it follow from *G*(*P*, *t*, *h*) that there is no other action *h'* for which there is a reason for *P* as well: *G*(*P*, *t*, *h'*)?

I shall try to show that the first question must be answered in the negative. I believe that the second question must also be answered in the negative, because besides *internal* reasons there do exist *external* reasons as well. External reasons are reasons for which it is not *analytically true* that they are at the same time motives of the agent. (The first question must be answered with 'no' not only for internal, but also for external reasons.)

The third question gives cause to introduce the term *'prima-facie'-reason*. There are situations in which reasons for or against a decision - or reasons for *h* and reasons for *h'* - must be weighed up. This weighing up finally results in a well-justified decision for one of the possible actions, e. g. for *h*. To the predicate 'well-justified' there corresponds a reason *G** for the respective action which is not compatible with a reason *G** for another well-justified action *h'*. The asterix * denotes that in this case the reasons we are talking about are not mere 'prima-facie'-reasons.

The usual interpretation of the Bayesian criterion implies that a rational person decides for *h*, *because h* maximizes the expected value of the subjective desirability. In this usual interpretation T1 would be a model of justification* of an action. The consequentialist character of this interpretation becomes clear, if we introduce the term *'consequentialist prima-facie-reason for an action'*. For a person *P*, *G* is a consequential (internal) prima-facie-reason for *h*, if *P* has a desire *Z*, and if *P* thinks that *Z* can be achieved by *h* (or, weakened: if *Z* is 'fostered' by *h* or 'is made probable - or at least more probable -' by *h*). This characterization of consequential reasons for actions can be trivialized by assigning a respective desire to any intentional action: the desire to perform this specific action. The desire to perform an action is, however, a conceptual element of every action: to act is to do something intentionally$_{O}$. In the consequentialist interpretation of T1 this kind of desire must therefore be excluded.

Even desires in the sense of *preceding intentions* cannot be taken into consideration, because the condition for the fulfillment of preceding intentions is - as has been shown in the last chapter - the respective action itself. The desire is directed towards a state *Z*, and *Z* is the goal of action *h*: To achieve *Z* is the *motivating intention* for the realization of *h*. The agent assumes that *Z* is a (sure, probable or at least possible) *consequence* of action *h* (of course the desire can also refer to consequences which are the *result* of *h*).

In comparison the fact that *h* belongs to a type of action *T* cannot be taken into consideration as a possible goal of this action. If *P* has the desire to say the truth, then *P* has a preceding intention which gets fulfilled if the respective speech act belongs to the type of action 'to make a true statement'. We can certainly assign to this intention, too, a desire which gets fulfilled by *h*. But the object of this desire is of a special kind: it does not refer to a state of the world as a consequence of the action, but it refers to something which is logically inseparable connected with the action itself. Here the model of an action which influences the future course of the world is no longer adequate: whether the desire has been satisfied or not cannot be seen from the state of the world, but from the kind of which the action itself is. The relation between the kind of the action and and a state of the world as a consquence of this action is, however, not an unambiguous one. The differentiation between and intrinsic and and extrinsic goods, first made by Aristotle, points into a similar direction. If a good the agent wants to achieve is not a consequence of the action, but a characteristic feature of the action itself, then the aspired good is inherent to the action, and does not belong to the state of the world which has possibly been evoked by it - accordingly, here the action itself is intrinsically good.

Consequentialist reasons for actions correspond to a specific type of motivating intentions, as have been introduced in the last chapter. There we have distinguished between motivating intentions which are directed towards a person's own actions (more precisely: which have as the condition for their fulfillment actions which are assumed to be consequences of a well-justified action) on the one hand, and motivating intentions which are not directed towards a person's own actions - which we have called 'simple' motivating intentions on the other hand. Consequentialist reasons of actions correspond to motivating intentions that do not in any way refer to features of the respective action itself or to features of any other actions which are realized by the agent herself.

Under the consequentialist interpretation of T1 the subjective valuation function, the expected value of which is maximized by the rational person, represents the variety of consequentialist prima-facie-reasons for possible actions: in this function all consequentialist prima-facie-reasons, weighed up and evaluated, have been taken up and result in a coherent overall valuation. *The subjective valuation function of T1 constitutes the (consequentialist) reason* for h*: *h* has the highest subjective value for *P* of all possible actions.

T2, on the other hand, cannot be interpreted as a model of internal and *a forteriori* not even as a model of *consequentialist* reasons for actions. None of the rationality postulates and no combination of these postulates of T2 implies a rational person's valuation of actions to assess only their consequences. Whether the postulates of T2 are satisfied exclusively depends on the form of the preference relation. Contrary to what might be assumed at first sight a consequentialist theory of rationality of action can, therefore, not be justified by the utility theorem. The standard consequentialist interpretation of T1 is not backed up by T2. T1 and T2 are equivalent only in so far as the subjective valuation function *u* of T1 can be regarded as a purely *numerical representation* of the consistent individual preference relation in the sense of T2. Any further specification regarding the content of this function *u* repeals the logical equivalence of T1 and T2. Any interpretation of *u* which does not take it as a pure metrification of the underlying preferences, but e. g. as an expression of the subjective valuation of states of the world, necessarily assigns an entirely different status to the claim that a rational person maximizes expected utility: under this kind of interpretation the thesis of the maximization of the expected value can no longer be justified by the coherence postulates of T2. A non-consequentialist theory of rational decision must, on the other hand, either show that at least one of the postulates of T2 is dispensable, or it must show how T1 can be interpreted in a non-consequentialist way.

## 3. Propositional Attitudes

Bayesian decision theory can be understood as to explicate rational action in terms of two types of propositional attitudes: wishing (desiring) and believing (presuming, assuming). Accordingly, the subjective valuation function over states of the world, propositions or events is interpreted as desirability, whereas the probability function represents the inclination of the individual to assume a (future) event to occur.[3] On the basis of the fact that actions are in one way or another (causally, logically, or in a particular 'third' way) connected with intentions, a reductionist theory of intentions is connected with Bayesian decision theory - reductionist insofar as it reduces the concept of rational intentions (as those intentions which are connected with a rational decision) to the concepts of desiring and believing.

The intentions we are addressing in this context are *preceding intentions* in the sense of chapter 3. Insofar we could regard decision theory as *a theory of rational preceding intentions in the face of given*

---

[3] There are, of course, other possibilities to describe and to interpret the basic concepts of decision theory: the probability function could, for example, be interpreted as the agent's assumption of certain probabilities - but this interpretation runs into difficulties as soon as unique events, which cannot just be repeated, are involved. In more complex conceptions the probability function, as employed in the Bayesian model, could also be interpreted as representing subjective assumptions about given probabilities and/or about a person's assumptions regarding objective probabilities. In the last case, objective probabilities could be maintained even without a frequentistic interpretation.

*subjective desires and assumptions*. A rational preceding intention is directed towards the action with the highest expected value, and, in case this action should not be possible, towards another action with the second highest expected value, etc.[4] The hierarchy resulting from this procedure is reflected in the numerical values of the function *u* which is on its part secured by the utility theorem.

Depending on the interpretation of decision theory as a normative, descriptive or explicative theory, this reduction will have the character of a normative, descriptive or conceptual claim. In the first case the key sentence of the theory is: a person *P should have* those preceding intentions which are, in the form defined by the theory, connected with her desires and assumptions; in the second case: a person *P has* these preceding intentions; and in the third case the *concept* of a preceding intention (in the form established by the theory) is explicated or ideally defined by the concepts of desiring and assuming.

The presupposition for a conception of decision theory as a reductionist theory of rationality is that the valuation functions (utility functions) which are to be optimized really are desirability functions, i. e. valuation functions reflecting the subjective desires of the agent in the sense of internal reasons. With actual persons this premise will certainly often or mostly not be true. The central question, however, is not whether this premise is or is not true with regard to actual persons, but whether we can assume that the desires of the ideally rational person (in the sense of the theory) are reflected in the subjective valuation functions of the Bayesian model. The opinion sometimes put forward that this question as such does not make any sense since the desires of a person are constituted only by means of test-questions etc. in the artificial process of the construction of a subjective valuation function, is based on an operationalist conception which is, at least in this case, misleading. A theory of the relation between desires and actions must prove to be adequate against the background of our pretheoretic comprehension.

The second critical question regarding T1 under the consequentialist interpretation is the following: is the relation between the desires

---

[4] If two actions have the same expected value, and if no other possible action has a higher expected value, then a rational intention can be directed towards each of these two actions, but not towards both of them simultaneously - the rational person will not behave like Buridan's donkey.

(and assumptions) of the agent on the one hand, and rational intentions (preceding intentions) on the other hand, represented in an adequate way? Is there really such a close relation between desires, assumptions and intentions as Bayesian consequentialism claims? For theory T1, if understood consequentialistically, the decision for an action out of a variety of optional actions is a choice of the best means. Goals of actions are subjective action-relevant desires and inclinations which in the concrete situation of a decision condense into (action-) motivating (consequentialist) intentions: therefore, the function *u* which is to be maximized represents the motivating intentions of the agent. Intrapersonally divergent *action-relevant* desires are weighed up against each other and united in a consistent valuation function which can be regarded as a quantitative representation of motivating intentions. In cases in which this procedure does not seem to be practicable - for some desires are *uncomparable* (e. g. the desires to stay alive and to go on an exciting trip on a motorbike) - this weighing up is carried out in the indirect way of a fictitious decision between uncertain alternatives (lotteries), i. e. in the way of T2. The fascination of Bayesian consequentialism explains itself by the elegance of this solution of the problem (even if it seems to be some kind of a 'platonizing model'): the coherence of the desirabilities is established by means of T2 and is reflected in a quantitative valuation function which can be assigned to the rational person.

It has been shown that, on the basis of the conditions of T2, T1 is not logically conclusive. But this alone can be no sufficient reason to condemn Bayesian consequentialism. Its inadequacy as a conception of rationality remains to be shown.

## 4. Self-oriented Consequentialism

In its interpretation of the basic terms the 'classical' model of decision theory proposed by L. J. Savage surprisingly commits itself definitely to a self-oriented consequentialist conception of rationality. In Savage's model the circumstances relevant for an action determine the consequences of the action (actions as functions of circumstances into consequences). Consequences, however, are here interpreted in a particular way: they are regarded as *"states of the [acting] person"*.[5] This model can, therefore, be used for the characterization of a specific version of consequentialism which we call *'self-oriented consequentialism'* (sc-version, and, accordingly: 'sc-better' and 'sc-rational'). *In the sense of self-oriented consequentialism a decision is rational, if there has been no other possible decision which would have improved the subjective state of the agent.*

It is rather irrelevant in terms of which valuation standards this *better*-relation over the subjective states is characterized; in almost every case this version of consequentialist rationality is far from being trivial. If in a situation $S$ for a person $P$ the action $h$ is an sc-rational action, then there does not exist any other possible $h'$ such that the subjective situation of $P$ as a consequence of $h'$ would be better than her subjective situation as a consequence of $h$ in $S$.[6] If $P$ wants to give a donation in order to do something against the misery in the Third World, she has a specific goal (to diminish misery), and as a rational person she considers which means will serve her best to attain this goal. She has the choice among a variety of organizations which - each with different measures - foster foreign aid projects in the countries of the Third World. Obviously, the goal of the decision - the motivating intention - is not directed towards an improvement of the subjective situation of the agent herself. The *criterion* of her choice is not self-oriented.

This action orientation, however, does nonetheless not exclude, as a consequence of the decision, a change in the subjective state of the person - she has a 'good conscience' now, for a certain time she will enjoy her relative affluence more relaxed. But, obviously, this aspect of the consequences of the action is no reason (or element of a justification) for the action, it could at best be taken into consideration as an element of a (causal) explanation. Among all possible actions one action can have the best subjective consequences without the improvement of the subjective situation being the criterion for the respective decision. It might well be that a pure altruist in such a way *de facto* optimizes his subjective situation. But it would nevertheless be in-

---

[5] Savage (1954), p. 14.

[6] An objectivist interpretation of this 'better-relation' is not excluded. One can think of objective standards that can be used in comparing subjective states, i. e. standards which do not depend on the judgment of the agent himself.

adequate to insinuate that the altruist acted sc-rationally: the improvement of the subjective situation is not the motive for his action.[7]

## 5. Consequentialism as a Model of Justification

To avoid misunderstandings we use the term 'consequentialism' in this context exclusively in the sense of a *model of justification*. It does, therefore, not suffice here to characterize the concept of rationality of self-oriented consequentialism by the descriptive means of the Savage-model. Only the actions which are performed on the basis of *preceding intentions* can be considered to be sc-rational. Central entities being subjected to criteria of rationality are patterns of behaviour or actions *in their combination with motivating intentions* (intentions$_m$). And as the fulfillment of a preceding intention can be thwarted by external constraints, it is even more appropriate to take as the actual object of evaluation the whole range of motivating and preceding intentions,[8] regardless of the fact that as well for an observer of the first kind mentioned above this range of intentions of course manifests itself in the actual performance of an action or in specific concrete and observable behaviour. Due to the close relation between intentions and actions or behaviour we have reason to speak of sc-rational agency as well, and moreover, we can even talk about sc-rational behaviour. There should not, of course, be left any doubt that this can only be allowed as a *façon de parler*, or more precisely: this can only be allowed if the con-

---

[7] This differentatiation seems to be the central idea in J. Butler's critique of egoism, cf. *Fifteen Sermons* (1726); C. D. Broad, (1930), ch. 3, and (1950). In our terminology: Psychological egoism mistakes a causal consequence of the fulfillment of a preceding intention for the motive for an action. Of course I am happy if my donation helps to diminish the misery in the Third World, but this being happy was not the motive for my decision. This can be condensed in the following thesis: the improvement of my subjective states is almost always just a consequence, and only very rarely a motive for actions I perform. Where the improvement of my subjective state is the immediate motive for a respective action, i. e. where it is the motivating intention, the action will only very rarely bring about the desired consequence, i. e. the improvement of my subjective state.

[8] It is not just accidentially so that we speak of 'decision theory', and not of a 'theory of rational action'. Decisions, however, are still no actions, and must in our terminology be identified with preceding intentions.

crete action in question is a condition for the fulfillment of a consequentialistically motivated preceding intention.

## 6. Actions of Intrinsic Value

One kind of critique of consequentialism opposes the idea that a decision for one specific alternative action is nothing but a *choice of means*. To put it in terms of the basic notion of consequentialism: an action *h* is consequentialistically rational if and only if the agent is aiming at something that he thinks to attain by means of *h*. More elaborated consequentialist theories also take into account subjective probabilities and conflicting goals, as Bayesian theory does by introducing the criterion of maximizing expected value in which the subjective valuation function is interpreted as representing motivating intentions.

But can this concept be applied to actions of intrinsic value as well? This question need not bother us if it was possible to show that *prima facie* intrinsically motivated actions can be reconstructed as extrinsically motivated actions. Let us have a look at the following example: *P* wants to express his thanks to *S* (*t*) and, in order to do this, he sends her a bunch of flowers. *P*'s action of sending flowers (*s*) certainly is extrinsically motivated: it is a means for *P* to express his thanks. *P* expresses his thanks by performing action *s*: *t* is a consequence (not a result!) of *s*. Performing *s* can of course be a rational choice of means, because under nearly all possible conditions *t* will be a consequence of *s* - let aside the hypothetical case that *P* cannot be sure whether his flowers really were delivered to *S*, so that e. g. in a country with an unreliable mail servive he would rather have chosen another action in order to realize *s*. *t* was the *reason* for *s*: *P* had the motivating intention *t* and believed that *s* was an appropriate means to fulfill *t*, so this is the reason why *P* did *s*. So far, this example fits very well into the consequentialist framework. But, obviously, *t* also is an action of *P*. The consequentialist reconstruction must therefore be carried on: what was the reason for *t*? This question *P* might answer by pointing out that in the future he will still have to rely on the help of *S* and that he hoped that as a result of *t* she will then still be well-disposed towards him (*w*). At this point the consequentialist analysis of the example would have come to a satisfactory end, because *w* is no longer an action of *P*. We could, of course, ask what makes *w* desirable for *P*, but the consequentialist analysis ends where we leave the realm of decisions and actions. But, on the other hand, it is likely that *P* answered to the question above that by doing *s* he intended nothing else but to express his thanks to *S*. In this case, there seems to be no other goal for which to attain *t* could be conceived as an appropriate means - in this case *t* is intrinsically motivated, or in other words: 'For *P*, *t* is an intrinsic goal' or '*t* is of intrinsic value for *P*'. Contrary to the consequentialist dogma, despite the lack of any action goal (and the conviction of the agent that *t* was an appropriate means to attain that goal) *t* seems to be perfectly well justified: Being asked another time about his reasons for doing *t*, *P* might answer: 'In the past, *S* often was a great help to me', and an answer of this kind seems indeed to express a sensible reason why *P* wants to express his thanks to *S*.

This example shows that there are intrinsically motivated actions which do not fit into the concept of Bayesian consequentialism. We now have to analyze whether this is true for all *intrinsically motivated*[9] actions - actions that have a specific value which does not exclusively depend on their respective *'ergon'*.[10] Independently from their consequences, actions not always but very often have a certain 'intrinsic value'. What is to be understood by 'value' can for the moment be left open to subjective interpretation. The performance of an action itself can e. g. be pleasureful. E. g., one does not only eat in order not to be hungry any more, the act of eating itself can be pleasureful. Within the framework of a consequentialist analysis the *intrinsic* value of an action becomes a feature of the consequences of the action, part of the value function which is to be maximized. A somewhat clumsy linguistic illustration of such an example is the following: 'One eats steak *in order* to have pleasure'. The state of pleasure must here, however, be

---

9 Whoever, being in favour of an objectivist interpretation, wants to avoid terms like 'of intrinsic value', may replace it by the term 'intrinsically motivated'. So do, for example, Audi (1986) and Mele (1988).

10 The first sentences of Aristotle's Nicomachean Ethics are the following: "Every *techne* ('art') and every *episteme* ('investigation', 'knowledge', 'science'), and similarly every *praxis* ('action') and *proairesis* ('pursuit'), is considered to aim at some good. Hence the Good has been rightly defined as 'that at which all things aim". Clearly, however, there is some difference between the *teloi* ('ends') at which they aim: some are *energeiai* ('activities') and other *erga* ('results') distinct from the activities' (1094a).

conceptually distinguished from the state of eating (that is from the specific pleasure to eat a steak), it must be distinguished from the action of eating which here is only the means chosen in order to attain pleasure. But whereas on the one hand it does not seem to pose any problem to understand what it means to enjoy eating steaks, on the other hand, it appears to be quite difficult to distinguish between the action as such and the adverbial characterization of its subjective value, because the results we get in this kind of analysis are abstract states of mind or conditions that are difficult to grasp: the goal of eating a steak would then be to attain a specific state of mind, that is to get pleasure - *per se*. In this case, I do not order steak because I like to eat steaks, but because I try to attain a specific state of mind that is a consequence of this action. It is remarkable that adverbial formulations for the description of specific personal preferences indeed baulk at a separation of two different conditions or processes - of eating, e. g., on the one hand, and of having pleasure on the other.

A consequentialist analysis taking into account the *intrinsic value* of an action would, therefore, need to dismantle actions of intrinsic value into an object of decision that has no value for itself on the one hand, and the result of the respective decision which then has a specific value on the other. This procedure is highly artificial. Basically, it leads to the result that in a consequentialist analysis, the intrinsic motivation of an action can only be grasped by giving a new description 'in terms of which' the action can then again be defined as extrinsically motivated. But this, of course, is only a shift of the problem of intrinsic motivation. We can therefore stick to the claim that actions of intrinsic value can be well-justified. It would, therefore, be inappropriate to exclude them from the application of a theory of rational behaviour. But actions of intrinsic value cannot be *conseqentialistically rational*.

## 7. Rules and Consequences

A particularly interesting case of application of this demand to dismantle actions into an object of intention (without intrinsic value) on the one hand, and the result of the respective action (with a specific value) on the other, is rule-following. If a person $P$ in a specific situation utters something ($A$) which is true, then it is a *consequence* of this (speech-)act *h* that *P* has been truthful, and that, accordingly, *P* has not told a lie: *h* fulfills the rule of truthfulness RT. If asked for the reason for *h*, *P* could answer: 'This (concrete) action *h* fulfills the rule RT' or just 'I did not want to lie'. If, in the respective situation, the only choice *P* had was to decide between two possibilities, to say either *A* or $\neg A$ (*h*'), then he has obviously chosen that possibility which was the only one corresponding to his goal - to say the truth. The question now is: Did *P* act consequentialistically rational when he chose to do *h*?

Let us first have a look at self-oriented consequentialism. It might be that *P*'s motivating intention for doing *h* was to follow the rule RT, but it might just as well be that the reason why *P* had this *motivating intention* was another intention, e. g. the intention to avoid trouble. It might, therefore, also be the case that *P* has decided in favour of *h* because it promised to have better subjective consequences for him than *h'*. In this case, *P* would have acted sc-rationally. But finally, it might also be that *P* cannot give any further explanation for having decided for *h* and that he insists on having had no other goal than simply to follow the rule RT. If we assume that this really is the case - would *P* even then have acted sc-rationally? It might be that because of his decision for doing *h*, *P* now must face certain disadvantages which he would not have to face if he had decided for *h'*. In this case, *P*'s decision for *h* would not be sc-rational. But could *h* even then remain a *consequentialistically rational* action, even if it turned out to be not sc-rational?

It is important to see *that the consequentialist notion of rationality would be totally trivial if mere conformity of an action to a rule was sufficient to characterize the action as consequentialistically rational, given that the conforming to the rule was the only motivating intention of the agent.* It is necessary to dissociate consequentialism from this trivialization. Whereas, as we have seen above, the self-oriented version of consequentialism is immune to such trivialization if it is understood as a model of justification (the criterion of action *h* is the subjective situation of the agent, the 'consequences' in the Savage-model), the dissociation of consequentialism in its unspecific form must be supported by a model in which actions are characterized as a choice of one branch at a certain point of ramification of the tree. The different branches of the tree symbolize the respective consequences of different states of the world.

In this model, the consequences of an action are nothing else but a *specific distribution of probabilities* on the twigs of the branch that has been chosen at the point of ramification. But we did not go into any further analysis of the question what belongs to the characteristic features of a state of the world and what could be understood as its ideal, that is complete description. Now just suppose that the concrete utterance *A* in the example given above takes place at one single point of time *t*. Exactly this is the moment of the transition from $z_i$ to $z_{i+1}$. In this very moment *t*, *P* decides in favour of *h* and against *h'*: he has determined the successive state $z_{i+1}$. The fact that *A* is true is not part of the characteristic features of $z_{i+1}$, it does, therefore, neither belong to the features of the branch that symbolizes the consequences of action *h*. That *A* is true characterizes *h* itself, it is a characteristic feature of *h* that *A* is true. A state of the world is interpreted as a complete conjunction of generic facts. Therefore it is not unique: any state of the world could just as well be an element of another branch of the tree. Accordingly, the mode or way in which the transition from $z_i$ to $z_{i+1}$ takes place cannot be element of $z_{i+1}$ itself. This is intuitively plausible as well, because given that one can have any clear intuition about the identity of possible worlds at all, two states of the world will certainly not be different just for the reason that one of them emerged from the preceding state by means of a lie whereas the other one did not. In other words: it is perfectly possible to imagine two totally identical states of the world that nonetheless have two different past histories. Whether they came into being by means of a lie or because the respective person told the truth does not bother, it does not belong to their actual existence, but remains a part of their past histories.

CHAPTER 5

# Formal Economic Rationality

A set of decisions or a person's preference relation over actions is coherent only if there exists a probability function over the set of events as well as a subjective utility function over the set of consequences, such that the (subjective) expected utility of the preferred decision is, in each case, higher than that of the non-preferred decision.[1]

Consequently, as a first step, we can characterize rational behaviour as a behaviour which is in accordance with coherent individual preferences. Quite contrary to what might be assumed at first sight, this is a conceptually clear definition, provided that it does not exclude stronger criteria of rationality and a restriction of its range of application. According to this definition, rational behaviour in situations of risk follows the Bayesian criterion of rationality which recommends to rank alternatives of action according to the respective degree of the expected value of subjective utility.[2]

There are various decision-theoretic models in terms of which the Bayesian criterion of rationality can be stated.[3] We do not want to discuss these models here.[4] Nonetheless, we shall outline a basic model which is suitable for an explication of rational behaviour in situations of risk (without interaction).

## 1. States of Affair and States of the World

'State of affair' is a basic concept which is relevant not only for decision theory, but also for probability theory and for collective choice theory.

---

[1] See Jeffrey (1965a), p. 533 f.

[2] There are many good introductions to rational decision theory, especially to the theory of decisions under risk. See e. g. Chernoff/Moses (1959), Luce/Suppes (1963), Raiffa (1978).

[3] See especially the theories of Savage (1954), Jeffrey (1967) and Fishburn (1964, 1966, 1970, 1972)

[4] For a detailed analysis of different models of decisions see Spohn (1978) and also Stegmüller (1973).

Savage defines a 'state of affairs' as 'a description of the world, leaving no relevant aspect undescribed'.[5] Jeffrey tries to explain the concept in the following way:

'Let us call a nonempty set of sentences a *novel*. The novel is *consistent* if the sentences that constitute it do not logically contradict each other; and a novel is *complete* if no sentence of the language could be added to it without rendering it inconsistent. Equivalently, a complete, consistent novel is a set of sentences which contains exactly one of each contradictory pair of sentences in the agent's language.

A complete, consistent novel describes a *possible world* [...] in as much detail as is possible without exceeding the resources of the agent's language. But if talk of possible worlds seems dangerously metaphysical, we can focus attention on the novels themselves and speak of a complete, consistent novel as actually being a possible world'.[6]

In the various decision-theoretic models the notion of 'states of affairs' has different tasks. In our model, the rôle of 'states of affairs' or 'possible worlds' is crucial: We assume that the individual subjective valuation functions (utility functions) $\upsilon_\iota$ are defined over the set of states of affairs: $\upsilon_\iota : \Xi \ni \xi \to x \in I\!R$.

## 2. Events

Events are sets of states (of affairs). The set of events is the power set of $\Xi$: $E := \mathrm{Pot}(\Xi)$. An event is the set of all those states in which the relevant proposition is true. $E$ is $\sim\cap\cup$-closed, i. e. the following conditions are satisfied:

(1) $\varepsilon \in E \Rightarrow \sim\varepsilon \in E$.

(2) $\varepsilon, \varepsilon' \in E \Rightarrow \varepsilon \cap \varepsilon' \in E$.

---

[5] Savage (1954), p. 9. Strictly speaken, however, we have no assumptions about subjective probabilities and about subjective desirabilities of *descriptions* but rather of the *described*.

[6] Jeffrey (1967), p. 208.

(3) $\varepsilon, \varepsilon' \in E \Rightarrow \varepsilon \cup \varepsilon' \in E$.[7]

$\varepsilon \cap \varepsilon'$ is the event which occurs if both $\varepsilon$ and $\varepsilon'$ occur at the same time. $\varepsilon \cup \varepsilon'$ is the event which occurs if at least one of the two events $\varepsilon$ and $\varepsilon'$ occurs. $\sim\varepsilon$ is the event which occurs if $\varepsilon$ does not occur: $\sim\varepsilon = \Xi \backslash \varepsilon$. Two events are called opposing events if the following holds: $\varepsilon \cup \varepsilon' = \Xi \wedge \varepsilon \cap \varepsilon' = \varnothing$. This is the case if and only if $\varepsilon' = \sim\varepsilon$. Two events are called disjoint if $\varepsilon \cap \varepsilon' = \varnothing$. A set of events $M$ is called complete if the union set of all events of this set equals $\Xi$.

## 3. Situation of Decision

A situation of decision (in the narrow sense)[8] is characterized by seven factors:

$$< \iota, \Xi, U, C, \Sigma^{\iota}, \rho_{\iota}, \upsilon_{\iota} >$$

- $\iota$ is the agent.
- $\Xi$ is the set of states (of affairs).
- $U$ is a complete set[9] of disjoint events. The elements of $U$ are called circumstances $e$.
- $C$ is a set of events. The elements of $C$ we denote by $c$, $c'$ etc. or $c_{\iota\alpha}$, $c_{\iota\beta}$, $c_{\iota\gamma}$ etc.[10]
- $\Sigma^{\iota}$ is the set of alternative actions. $\Sigma^{\iota}$ is a set of functions mapping elements of $U$ onto elements of $C$. The elements of $\Sigma^{\iota}$ are referred to by $\sigma$, $\sigma'$, in the countable case by $\sigma_{\iota\alpha}$, $\sigma_{\iota\beta}$, $\sigma_{\iota\gamma}$ etc.
- $\rho_{\iota}$ is a subjective act-conditioned probability function over Pot($\Xi$).
- $\upsilon_{\iota}$ is a function over $\Xi$ in $\mathbb{R}$.

---

[7] $E$ is a Boolean algebra. See Jehle (1974).

[8] A decision situation in the narrow sense comprises situations under risk and certainty without interaction.

[9] We assume all sets to be finite and nonempty.

[10] $\alpha, \beta, \gamma \in \mathbb{N}$

## 4. A Decision Criterion

A decision criterion assigns two functions to every situation of decision $<\iota, \Xi, U, C, \Sigma^{\iota}, \rho_{\iota}, \upsilon_{\iota}>$
- a function $\hat{\upsilon}_{\iota}$ (subjective valuation of the consequences) from $C$ in $I\!R$ and
- a function $u_{\iota}$ (subjective valuation of the actions) of $\Sigma^{\iota}$ in $I\!R$.

Depending on the subjective valuation of the consequences, the decision rule assigns to every situation of decision $< \iota, \Xi, U, C, \Sigma^{\iota}, \rho_{\iota}, \upsilon_{\iota} >$ the following valuation function of the actions:

$$\text{(I)}\ u(\sigma) = \sum_{e \in U} \hat{\upsilon}_{\iota}(\sigma(e)) \cdot \rho_{\iota}(e|\sigma)$$

or, if $\rho_{\iota}(e)$ is not depending on the decision:

$$\text{(I')}\ u_{\iota}(\sigma) = \sum_{e \in U} \hat{\upsilon}_{\iota}(\sigma(e)) \cdot \rho_{\iota}(e).$$

This suggests to describe the interrelation between the consequences and the valuation of the circumstances in a similar way:

$$(*)\ \hat{\upsilon}_{\iota}(c) = \sum_{\xi \in c} \upsilon_{\iota}(\xi) \cdot \rho_{\iota}(\{\xi\}|\sigma).$$

But this would be inadeqate, because although for the probabilities of the states of affairs it is not true that

$$\sum_{e \in U} \rho_{\iota}(e|\sigma) = 1,$$

the following does not generally hold:[11]

$$\sum_{\xi \in c} \rho_{\iota}(\{\xi\}|\sigma) = 1.$$

---

[11] However, since the circumstances in a situation of decision are disjoint, it holds that $\forall e,e' \in U$: $\rho_{\iota}(e \cap e') = 0$ and $\forall \xi,\xi' \in c : \rho_{\iota}(\xi \cap \xi') = 0$.

This implies that the weighing of (*) gets distorted by the decision-conditioned total probability of $c$: $\rho_\iota(c|\sigma)$. Whereas (I) implies

$$\min(\{\hat{\upsilon}_\iota(\sigma(e))\}) \leq u(\sigma) \leq \max(\{\hat{\upsilon}_\iota(\sigma(e))\}),$$

it does not hold respectively, that

$$\min(\{\upsilon_\iota(\xi)\}) \leq \hat{\upsilon}(c) \leq \max(\{\upsilon_\iota(\xi)\}).$$

It is rather the case that

$$\min(\{\upsilon_\iota(\xi)\}) \cdot \sum_{\xi\in c} \rho_\iota(\{\xi\}|\sigma) \leq \upsilon_\iota(c) \leq \max(\{\upsilon_\iota(\xi)\}) \cdot \sum_{\xi\in c} \rho_\iota(\{\xi\}|\sigma),$$

and, therefore, (*) must be modified to

$$\text{(II)}\ \hat{\upsilon}_\iota(c) = \frac{\sum_{\xi\in c} \upsilon_\iota(\xi)\cdot\rho_\iota(\{\xi\}|\sigma)}{\sum_{\xi\in c} \rho_\iota(\{\xi\}|\sigma)} \quad \left(\text{with } \sum_{\xi\in c} \rho_\iota(\{\xi\}|\sigma) = \rho_\iota(c|\sigma)\right).$$

(II) resembles Jeffrey's definition of desirability for propositions.[12]

$$(**)\ \upsilon_\iota(p \cup p') = \frac{\upsilon_\iota(p)\cdot\rho_\iota(p) + \upsilon_\iota(p')\cdot\rho_\iota(p')}{\rho(p \cup p')}$$

(with $p$ and $p'$ being propositions).

It is important to see that (II) cannot be subjected to the same objections as (**),[13] since according to the definition of the situation of decision $\rho_\iota(c \cap c') = 0$ is true for all consequences $c$, $c'$ of an action satisfying $c = \sigma(e)$, $c' = \sigma(e')$ and $c \neq c'$.[14]

In most cases, however, it would be erroneous to suppose that $\iota$ could indeed have a subjective probability valuation for all possible

[12] See Jeffrey (1967), p. 80.

[13] See Spohn (1978), p. 77 ff.

[14] Where of course $e, e' \in U$ and, hereby, $e \neq e'$ - since $\sigma$ is a function.

worlds[15] from $C$. It is more realistic to assign to $\iota$ a probability valuation of some subsets of $C$ - making the idealizing assumption that $\iota$, within these subsets $c$, is at a complete loss which probabilities to assign to their respective elements.[16]

Therefore, a transition from the valuation of states of affairs to the valuation of consequences, which is more appropriate for application, consists in two steps:

1. Forming a complete set $M$ (complete w. r. t. $c$) of disjoint subsets of $c$

$$\forall \mu, \mu' \in M : \mu \cap \mu' = \varnothing \wedge \bigcup_{\mu \in M} \mu = c$$

such that $\iota$ has a subjective probability for all $\mu \in M$. The subjective valuation of the elements of $M$ could, then, be obtained via the rule

$$\tilde{\nu}_\iota(\mu) = \min(\{\nu_\iota(\xi) \xi \in \mu\})$$

The fragmentation of $c$ in $M$ could be oriented at the valuation function $\nu_\iota$ in so far as the elements of $M$ preferably comprise states which do not make a big difference (w. r. t. the valuation) to $\iota$.

2. The transition from $\tilde{\upsilon}_\iota$ to $\hat{\upsilon}_\iota$ would, once again, be 'Bayesian':

$$\hat{\upsilon}_\iota(c) = \sum_{\mu \in M} \tilde{\upsilon}_\iota(\mu) \cdot \rho_\iota(\mu | \sigma).$$

This approach differs from Savage's conception among other things in the following respects: the valuation of the consequences is a 'derived

[15] When we are, somewhat sloppy, talking about the subjective probability of a state, we do not mean $\rho_\iota(\xi)$ but $\rho_\iota(\{\xi\})$.
[16] More precisely: the subsets of $c$ being singletons.

valuation'[17], consequences and circumstances are sets of states of affairs, and, finally, consequences are interpreted objectivistically.[18]

Our approach is similar to Jeffrey's by virtue of the consequences and circumstances being subsets of $\Xi$. But there are two differences to Jeffrey's 'holistic' approach: first, in our model, actions are not subsets of $\Xi$, but rather, in the context of a given situation of decision, defined as functions from the set of circumstances into the set of consequences;[19] secondly, (and this is of special importance for our topic), in our model there is no primary valuation of propositions.

## 5. Propositions

We have already discussed the notion of a 'proposition' above. Wishes, desires, hopes, assumptions, suppositions refer to propositions. 'He wishes that the sun will shine tomorrow; she hopes that he will visit her; we assume that there exists no highest prime number'; we suppose that wishes refer to propositions.

'I wish more time and leisure' can also be expressed in the form of a proposition: 'I'd love to have more time and leisure'. Gramatically, objects of dispositions of belief or desire often are other things than propositions in everyday language. But all sentences of such a kind can, without any change in meaning, also be propositionally rephrased. Preferences (of whatever type) expressed in language always refer to propositions: 'This year she prefers Italy to Spain for her summer holidays' means that she prefers one proposition - to go on holiday to Italy this year - to another proposition - to go to Spain this year. And, similarly, almost every preference expressed in language can be propositionally interpreted.

---

[17] Analogously, we have in all decision models not a direct but a derived valuation of actions (which is relative to the valuation of the consequences and the probabilities).

[18] Consequences are not 'states of the person' or descriptions under characteristics which $\iota$ takes to be relevant for his/her utility.

[19] Hereby, we are satisfying Spohn's demand not to extend the definition of the probability function $\rho_\iota$ to alternative actions ($\Sigma^\iota$), see Spohn (1978), pp. 72-78.

How can propositions and propositional preferences be related to the concepts we have already introduced above?

Every proposition can be characterized by a set of states. In mathematical terms, therefore, it is possible to identify the set of propositions with the power set of $\Xi$, that is $\mathrm{Pot}(\Xi)$. As the subjective probability function $\rho_\iota$ is defined over the set of events, we can, in this way, assign a subjective probability to every proposition. Generally, however, this would be too much of an idealization. We have already weakened the degree of idealization by admitting restrictions of the set over which $\rho_\iota$ is defined to a subset of $\mathrm{Pot}(\Xi)$.[20]

If we do not only say that all propositions are elements of $\mathrm{Pot}(\Xi)$ (that is sets of possible worlds) but if we also say that every set of states corresponds to a proposition, we allow that propositions to exist which cannot be expressed in natural language: there is no guarantee that our language is rich enough to express whatever set of states of affairs with a sentence of the type: 'It is the case that...'.[21] Having this in mind, it appears to be more adequate to identify $\mathrm{Pot}(\Xi)$ with the set of facts. Then, every proposition corresponds to a fact, but at the same time there is not always a proposition for every fact. Analytically it can then remain true that every proposition corresponds to a sentence of the type 'It is the case that...'. We also have preferences concerning facts not corresponding to any proposition: often we do know exactly what we want, without being able to say exactly what we want.

Keeping this in mind we can now once again use the 'sloppy' way of speaking that identifies the set of propositions with $\mathrm{Pot}(\Xi)$. In this sense, circumstances and consequences are propositions, actions are not.[22]

---

[20] If one knows the subset of Pot($\Xi$) over which $\rho_\iota$ can reasonably be defined, one is still left with the choice to choose from different partitions of Pot($\Xi$) resp. $c$, the elements of which belong to the set over which $\rho_\iota$ is defined. Naturally, not *every* subset of Pot($\Xi$) allows for such a partition, but we can demand every set over which a subjective probability function is defined to have this property.

[21] To this rethoric question, there is even another answer apart from 'nobody', namely 'Jeffrey' - cf. the quoted passage above, in which states are identified with *complete novels*. We should not accept this identification, however, since with it language would be assumed to have to strong a function in 'making up the world'.

[22] Of course, a person can describe her own actions propositionally; however, in our model they are not an element of the set of events, but functions from $U$ to $C$,

Whereas the desirability of consequences remains uncertain and depends on the subjective probabilities, one can well imagine that the desirability of states can be defined independent from any probabilities (and from other epistemic premises concerning the world as it is), at least in the weaker form of a ranking or an ordinal valuation. We might say: the smaller the set of states, the more precise is the subjective valuation.[23] The larger the set of states of affairs, the less possibility there is to make a sensible judgment about the subjective valuation of the respective proposition. With the subjective valuation of probability things are converse: the larger the set of states of affairs, the easier it is to assign a subjective probability to it.

Debreu[24] has shown that in the case of a situation of certainty[25] the postulate of utility maximizing behaviour can be deduced from two other postulates: the postulate of the connectedness of the individual preference ordering in the space of commodities $\mathbb{R}^m$ (which corresponds to our $\Xi$) and the postulate of the continuity of individual preference orderings:

(1) *Connectedness:* Weak individual preferences constitute a complete ordering over $\Xi$.

(2) *Continuity:* Let $\xi_1, \xi_2, \xi_3, \ldots$ be a sequence of states converging to $\xi_0$ (Debreu takes the states (=situations) to be points in the $m$-dimensional space of commodities $\mathbb{R}^m$.) and let $\xi_1', \xi_2', \xi_3', \ldots$ be another sequence of states converging to $\xi_0'$. If $\xi_\kappa \underset{\iota}{\geq} \xi_\kappa'$ for $\forall \kappa = 1, 2, 3, \ldots$, then: $\xi_0 \geq \xi_0'$.[26]

---

by which we avoid the problem of singling out specific types of propositions from the set over which the subjective probability function is defined.

[23] This is true for two sets $\mu$ and $\mu'$ from Pot($\Xi$), if $\mu \subset \mu'$ and $\#\mu < \#\mu'$ and not for arbitrary sets $\mu, \mu' \in$ Pot($\Xi$):
$\#\mu < \#\mu'$.

[24] See Debreu (1959), pp. 55-59.

[25] $\forall e \in U \; \forall \sigma \in \Sigma^\iota: p_\iota(e|\sigma) \in \{0,1\}$.

[26] Sometimes, these two axioms are called 'basic utility axioms', see Harsanyi (1979).

If the decision behaviour of an individual person satisfies the postulates (1) and (2), then each of her decisions maximizes a well-defined ordinal or cardinal utility function $\upsilon_l$. However, it is questionable one find good reasons establishing the status of these two postulates.

In the case of decisions under risk it is necessary to add two further postulates of rationality in order to be able to derive the Bayesian postulate of rational decisions:

(3) *Probabilistic equivalence of lotteries.* An agent is indifferent between two lotteries if their respective outcomes and probabilities are completely equal, independent from the type of random events and from the random mechanism employed.[27]

(4) *Choice of the dominant decision.* If the probabilities of the circumstances are independent from the decision and if the consequences of the circumstances are for one decision in any case better than for another decision, then the first of the two alternative decisions will be chosen.

Taken together, these four postulates only allow behaviour maximizing subjective (cardinal) value or utility.

Behaviour is coherent, if there is a probability function and a value function that describe every decision as one which maximizes the subjective value. Coherent behaviour can still be irrational. We consider a decision to be irrational, although it is maximizing the expected subjective utility with regard to the subjective probabilities and valuations of the agent if, for example, these probabilities are irrational (e. g. considering the agent's experience with a relative frequency of an event in the past). This can be the case even if the subjective probabilities satisfy the Kolmogoroff-axioms.

---

[27] A lottery is a chance experiment with known probabilities and outcomes associated to the probabilties:
$<\rho(e_1) \mid \pi(e_1), \rho(e_2) \mid \pi(e_2), \rho(e_3) \mid \pi(e_3), \ldots, \rho(e_n) \mid \pi(e_n)>$ with $\rho(e_k \cap e_l) = 0$ for $k, l \in \{1, 2, \ldots, n\}$, $k \neq l$, and $\sum_{k=1}^{n} \rho(e_k) = 1$.

An irrationality in the valuation of consequences is not excluded as well. The rationality of desires and wishes is a question addressed in 'cognitive psychology'. In his book *A Theory of the Good and the Right*, R. B. Brandt[28] describes some types of irrational valuations, 'erroneous' wishes, aims and aversions.

Finally, we also want to call a decision irrational if the agent does not make use of informations which do not 'cost' him anything in comparison to the possible damage resulting from a defective or wrong valuation.[29] Again, this aspect is independent from the coherence of the agents behaviour.[30]

## 6. Uncertainty

Up to this point we have dealt with individual rational behaviour in situations in which it makes sense to make a (decision-conditioned) valuation of the probabilities of the circumstances - $\rho_\iota(e|\sigma), e \in U$. We shall now address the question which sort of behaviour can be individually rational in situations in which a subjective assessment of the probabilities of the circumstances is impossible. Decision situations of this kind are *situations of uncertainty in the narrow sense*. If the agent when making her decision knows which circumstance will obtain, we call that a situation of certainty. In case the agent only has a subjective valuation of the probabilities of the circumstances, we call that a situation of risk. Finally, if the agent is not even capable of the subjective valuation that was still managable in the situation of risk, we are dealing with a situation of uncertainty in the narrow sense.

---

[28] See Brandt (1979), ch. VI, and Stegmüller (1977).

[29] For this issue, see Gärdenfors (1979).

[30] Coherent behaviour does not have to be rational, but one can expect an adequate concept of consistency to support the implication that rational behaviour is consistent. It is unclear as to whether the Bayesian concept of consistency allows for this as Allais' critique of Bayesianism has shown. See Allais (1953) and for the subsequent discussion Allais/Hagen (1979). The departing point is that persons systematically violated the Bayesian axioms of consistency when taking part in experiments (see also Schneeweiß (1967), p. 79).

Situations of certainty and situations of risk are different only with respect to the value of the (conditioned) subjective probability function over $U$. If 1 is among the values of the function, we are in the realm of decisions under certainty, if the value of the function never equals one, we are dealing with a situation of risk. In a situation of uncertainty, there is no probability function at all. Here it becomes clear that, without actually having named it then, we have already dealt with situations of uncertainty above, because we did not restrict the value space of $\rho$ to $[0,1)$. However, the model presented above is not suitable to represent situations of uncertainty.

In application, there are no clear boundaries between situations of risk and situations of certainty. This transition is reflected in the criteria of decision insofar as a situation of certainty turns into a borderline-case.

It is much more difficult to clarify the relation between situations of risk (including the case of certainty) on the one hand, and situations of uncertainty on the other. In a decision situation in which it appears to be useful to assign objective, but unknown probabilities to the circumstances, the agent is able to make conjectures about intervals these probabilities will lie in. If the agent believes that she knows the objective probabilites - e. g. in a situation in which she has to choose between two or more lotteries - then we have a clear case of a situation of risk. If, however, the agent is at a complete loss and does not have any idea about the objective probabilities, the situation is one of uncertainty.[31]

Let us imagine a strictly deterministic world. In other words: if in this world at a time $t_0$ the state of the world is $\xi_0$, then hereby all other states of this world $\xi(t)$ are definitely determined (for all $t$, $t>t_0$ and $t<t_0$). Additionally, the description of the states does not contain statistical propositions (i. e. every statistical proposition can be replaced by a set of non-statistical propositions). Are there objective probabilities in such a world?

Of course, even in a world like this, there are relative frequencies. But probabilities, however, are an 'expression of deficient knowledge'. In a deterministic world, statements about probabilities are obviously

[31] One can see that metatheoretical questions of probability theory bear upon the question which criterion for situations under ignorance one accepts, since a subjectivist (w. r. t. probabilities) probably would reject the proposal.

not about nature, but about a subjective expectation referring to given informations. It is not relevant how extensive these informations are. In any case we have, relative to the given information, an attitude of expectation which, accordingly, finds expression in corresponding subjective probabilities. Therefore, from a subjectivist point of view, the distinciton between a situation of risk and a situation of uncertainty cannot simply be taken for granted. A subjectivist could indeed argue against it, insisting that there is always a 'degree in strength of belief'.

Accordingly, a possible consequence of the subjectivist way of dealing with probabilities is to stick to the Bayesian decision criterion and to assume equal subjective probabilities in situations in which due to deficient information there is no reason to assume that one event is more probable than another. This results in the

*Laplace-criterion*: Prefer a decision $\sigma_K$ to a decision $\sigma_\lambda$ if and only if

$$\sum_{e \in U} \hat{\upsilon}_\iota(\sigma_\kappa(e)) > \sum_{e \in U} \hat{\upsilon}_\iota(\sigma_\lambda(e)).$$

There are two possible interpretations of the Laplace-criterion:

(1) The 'Bayesian' interpretation: If one has no reason to assume one of the circumstances (independent from the decision made) to be more probable than another, then, obviously, one assumes that these circumstances are equally true. In this case, the Bayesian decision rule is equivalent to the Laplace-criterion.

(2) If one does not have any information about the probabilities, one has to base the decision only upon the subjective valuation of the consequences. There is no reason why one of these consequences should be considered more strongly than others, and hence the sum of the utility of the possible consequences of an action is decisive.

Apart from these two interpretations, other criteria for a rational decision in a situation of uncertainty have been proposed.

The *maximin-criterion*[32]: Prefer a decision $\sigma_\kappa$ to a decision $\sigma_\lambda$ if and only if

$$\min(\{\hat{\upsilon}_\iota(\sigma_\kappa(e))\}) > \min\{(\hat{\upsilon}_\iota(\sigma_\lambda(e))\},\ e \in U$$

(i. e.: choose that decision for which the utility of the most disadvantageous consequence is maximal).

(I)

| | $e_1$ | $e_2$ | $e_3$ |
|---|---|---|---|
| $\sigma_1$ | 2 | 8 | 12 |
| $\sigma_2$ | 4 | 3 | 4 |
| $\sigma_3$ | 15 | 6 | 0 |

maximin $(\sigma_1) = 2$
maximin $(\sigma_2) = 4$
maximin $(\sigma_3) = 0$
$\sigma_2 > \sigma_1 > \sigma_3$

This criterion is less convincing in situations of decision in which there are only small differences in the valuation of the most disadvantageous consequences, but big differences in the valuation of other consequences.

(II)

| | $e_1$ | $e_2$ |
|---|---|---|
| $\sigma_1$ | 0,99 | 10 |
| $\sigma_2$ | 1 | 1 |

maximin $(\sigma_2) >$ maximin $(\sigma_1)$

---

[32] This is also called *Wald-criterion*, see Wald (1950).

The critique resulting from this provides the motivation for the

*Minimax-regret-criterion*:[33] Prefer a decision $\sigma_{\kappa}$ to a decision $\sigma_{\lambda}$ if and only if

$$-\max(\{\max(\{\hat{\upsilon}(\sigma_{\mu}(e_{\omega})) - \hat{\upsilon}(\sigma_{\kappa}(e_{\omega}))\})_{\mu}\})_{\omega} >$$
$$-\max(\{\max(\{\hat{\upsilon}(_{\mu}(e_{\omega})) - \hat{\upsilon}(\sigma_{\lambda}(e_{\omega}))\})_{\mu}\})_{\omega}$$

or: Choose the decision for which the maximal regret (compared with other possible decisions) is minimal.

(III)

| | $e_1$ | $e_2$ |
|---|---|---|
| $\sigma_1$ | 0,99 | 10 |
| $\sigma_2$ | 1 | 1 |

——> regret matrix

| | $e_1$ | $e_2$ |
|---|---|---|
| $\sigma_1$ | 0,01 | 0 |
| $\sigma_2$ | 0 | 9 |

MIMAR($\sigma_1$) = -0,01; MIMAR($\sigma_2$)= -9

(IV)

| | $e_1$ | $e_2$ | $e_3$ |
|---|---|---|---|
| $\sigma_1$ | 3 | 7 | 4 |
| $\sigma_2$ | 10 | 2 | 6 |
| $\sigma_3$ | 1 | 4 | 12 |

| | $e_1$ | $e_2$ | $e_3$ |
|---|---|---|---|
| $\sigma_1$ | 7 | 0 | 8 |
| $\sigma_2$ | 0 | 5 | 6 |
| $\sigma_3$ | 9 | 3 | 0 |

(regret matrix)

MIMAR ($\sigma_1$) = -8
MIMAR ($\sigma_2$) = -6
MIMAR ($\sigma_3$) = -9

$\sigma_2 > \sigma_1 > \sigma_3$

---

33 See Savage (1951).

According to the minimax-criterion in situation (II) decision $\sigma_2$ is rational. The minimax-regret-criterion, on the other hand, recommends $\sigma_1$, which seems to be more in accordance with our intuitions.

Whereas the maximin-criterion only considers the most disadvantageous of all possible consequences, the *maximax-criterion* only considers the best consequence of a decision:

*Maximax-criterion*. Prefer a decision $\sigma_\kappa$ to a decision $\sigma_\lambda$ if and only if

$$\max(\{\hat{\upsilon}(\sigma_\kappa|e_\mu))\})_\mu > \max(\{\hat{\upsilon}(\sigma_\lambda|e_\mu))\})_\mu$$

(i. e.: choose the decision for which the utility of the best consequence is maximal).

Between these two extremes which only consider either the most disadvantageous or the best consequence in the minimax- or the maximax-criterion, there is a continuum of decision rules. This continuum is characterized by the

*Hurwicz-criterion*:[34] Prefer a decision $\sigma_\kappa$ to a decision $\sigma_\lambda$ if and only if

$$r \min(\{\hat{\upsilon}(\sigma_\kappa|e_\mu)\})_\mu + (1\text{-}r) \max(\{\hat{\upsilon}(\sigma_\kappa(e_\mu))\})_\mu >$$
$$r \min(\{\hat{\upsilon}(\sigma_\lambda|e_\mu)\})_\mu + (1\text{-}r) \max(\{\hat{\upsilon}(\sigma_\lambda(e_\mu))\})_\mu, \text{ with } r\in[0,1].$$

For the definition of $r$ (optimism-pessimism-index) a decision situation is useful in which the index $r$ can be inferred from $x$, when the agent is indifferent between the two decisions $\sigma_1$ and $\sigma_2$ for a certain value $c$:

[34] See Luce/Raiffa (1957), S. 282 ff.

(V)

| | $e_1$ | $e_2$ |
|---|---|---|
| $\sigma_1$ | $\hat{\upsilon}(a)$ | $\hat{\upsilon}(b)$ |
| $\sigma_2$ | $\hat{\upsilon}(x)$ | $\hat{\upsilon}(x)$ |

without loss of generality: $\hat{\upsilon}(a) > \hat{\upsilon}(b)$.

$$r\ \hat{\upsilon}(a) + (1\text{-}r)\ \hat{\upsilon}(b) = r\ \hat{\upsilon}(x) + (1\text{-}r)\ \hat{\upsilon}(x) \Rightarrow r = \frac{\hat{\upsilon}(x) - \hat{\upsilon}(b)}{\hat{\upsilon}(a) - \hat{\upsilon}(b)}.$$

Presupposing that the *dominance-criterion* is not violated, there is an optimism-pessimism-index for every individual decision. Given a valuation function $\hat{\upsilon}$, this index, following the Hurwicz-rule, rationalizes any such decision. However, there is not a constant index corresponding to every preference relation over the set of decisions.

E. g., decision preferences that follow the minimax-regret-criterion do not have the same index which would make them rational according to the Hurwicz-rule.

If a person is acting according to the Laplace-criterion, she has an optimism-pessimism-index of 0.5, since she is indifferent between $\sigma_1$ and $\sigma_2$, if and only if in situation (V) the following is true:

$$0.5\,\hat{\upsilon}(a) + 0.5\,\hat{\upsilon}(b) = 0.5\,\hat{\upsilon}(x) + 0.5\,\hat{\upsilon}(x).$$

Herewith $x = 0.5\ (\hat{\upsilon}(a)+\hat{\upsilon}(b))$ and $r = \dfrac{\hat{\upsilon}(x) - \hat{\upsilon}(b)}{\hat{\upsilon}(a) - \hat{\upsilon}(b)} = 0.5$.

A person acting according to the maximax-criterion has the optimism-pessimism-index 1, since she is indifferent between $\sigma_1$ and $\sigma_2$ if and only if $\hat{\upsilon}(x) = \hat{\upsilon}(a)$.

A person acting according to the maximin-criterion has an optimism-pessimism index of 0, since she is indifferent between $\sigma_1$ and $\sigma_2$ if and only if $\hat{\upsilon}(x) = \hat{\upsilon}(b)$.

A decision according to the Laplace-criterion is rational with regard to an optimism-pessimism-index of 0.5, analogously a decision according to the maximin-criterion is rational with regard to an index of 0, etc.

In a behaviouristic model with a time-dependent index value any decision which has actually been choosen can, in the sense of Hurwicz, be said to be rational. Therefore, in such a model, one either needs some assumptions about a certain temporal invariability, or one has to modify the application of the criterion of rationality, applying it not to individual decisions, but to relations of decisions. Preference orderings over actions are only determined by decision behaviour, if a certain temporal invariability of the individual preferences can be presupposed.

Milnor has shown that in situations of uncertainty all these criteria of rational decision that we have listed above conflict with certain intuitively convincing minimal conditions.[35] A pure situation of uncertainty might be considered as a borderline-case in which the agent's information is too insufficient to determine the individual rationality of her decision behaviour. However, actual situations of decision, in general, can never be interpreted as pure situations of uncertainty or as pure situations of risk. Therefore, a theory of rational decision should develop a general criterion of rationality that produces as its borderline-cases on the one hand a decision criterion for risk, and on the other hand a decision criterion for uncertainty. A general criterion of such a kind could also much more easily be tested against intuitive desiderata.

To every circumstance we do not assign a probability, but a probability interval $I_\rho(e|\sigma)$.

$$\forall e \in U: I_\rho(e|\sigma) \subset [0,1].$$

[35] See Milnor (1954). Not all of the ten metacriteria for rational decision listed by Milnor can claim a selective function, the remaining rather serve for characterizing competing criteria.

In a case of risk the length of these intervals

$$\max(I_{\rho}(e|\sigma)) - \min(I_{\rho}(e|\sigma))$$

shrinks to zero (or at least nearly to zero). In a case of uncertainty the interval expands up to its maximal extension

$$\max(I_{\rho}(e|\sigma)) - \min(I_{\rho}(e|\sigma)) = 1.$$[36]

As a general criterion of rational decision Gärdenfors proposes the 'maximin criterion for expected utilities': in a situation of decision somewhere in between the two borderline-cases, a possible expected utility value would be:

$$\sum_{e \in U} \hat{\upsilon}_{\iota}(\sigma(e)) \cdot \rho(e|\sigma), \text{ in which } \forall e \in U: \rho(e|\sigma) \in I_{\rho}(e|\sigma).$$

The maximin-criterion of expected utilities reads: the decision $\sigma$ maximizing the minimal expected utility value is rational .

Herewith the desired is fulfilled: criteria of rational behaviour in pure situations of risk and in pure situations of uncertainty result as borderline cases from a general criterion of rationality. This is shown by the following operation:

$$(1)\ \lim_{\|I\rho\|^* \to 0} \min\left(\left\{\sum_{e \in U} \hat{\upsilon}_{\iota}(\sigma(e)) \cdot \rho(e|\sigma)\right\}\right)_{\rho(e|\sigma) \in I_{\rho}(e|\sigma)} = \sum_{e \in U} \hat{\upsilon}_{\iota}(\sigma(e)) \cdot \rho(e|\sigma)$$

in which $\|I_{\rho}(e|\sigma)\| = \max(I_{\rho}(e|\sigma)) - \min(I_{\rho}(e|\sigma))$;[37]

$$\|I_{\rho}\|^* = \max(\{\|I_{\rho}(e|\sigma)\|\})_{e \in U}$$

and

[36] Other then Gärdenfors (see Gärdenfors 1979), we also assume intervals of probability conditioned by actions.

[37] If there is no minimum in $I_{\rho}(e|\sigma)$, then we use the largest lower bound: $\inf(I_{\rho}(e|\sigma))$. Analogously for $\max(I_{\rho}(e|\sigma))$.

$$(2)\ \lim_{\|I_\rho\|^0 \to 1} \min\left(\left\{\sum_{e\in U} \hat{\upsilon}_\iota(\sigma(e))\cdot\rho(e|\sigma)\right\}\right)_{\rho(e|\sigma)\in I_\rho(e|\sigma)} = \min\left(\left\{\hat{\upsilon}_\iota(\sigma(e))\right\}\right)_{e\in U}$$

in which $\|I_\rho\|^0 = \min(\{\|I_\rho(e|\sigma)\|\})_{\varepsilon\in U}$.

Probability intervals can be interpreted as borderline-cases of second-order probabilities: my (subjective) probability for $\rho(e|\sigma)$ being outside of $I_\rho(e|\sigma)$ is 0, and my (subjective) probability for

$$\rho(e|\sigma)\in I_\rho(e|\sigma)$$

is 1. Of course, such second-order probabilities only make sense if $\rho(e|\sigma)$ is interpreted as an objective probability. Things become more complicated if these second-order probabilities are continuous, which probably is to be assumed as the normal case. Gärdenfors offers an interesting proposal for this. He proposes to substitute the probability intervals by so-called confidence intervals. For every circumstance $e$ the confidence interval $\tilde{I}_\rho(\sigma|e)$ is continued such that the (second-order) probability for the real (objective) probability of $e$ is an element of $\tilde{I}_\rho(\sigma|e)$ equals a quantity $\alpha\in[0,1]$. The larger the chosen quantity of $\alpha$, the greater is the risk aversion of the agent. It is possible to show that in the borderline-case of $\alpha = 0$ this '$\alpha$-maximin-criterion' is equivalent to the Bayesian criterion, and that in the borderline case $\alpha = 1$ (if all second-order probabilities for whatever objective probabilities are positive) it is equivalent to the usual maximin-criterion. It is interesting that this approach does not grasp such criteria as the maximax-criterion and the Hurwicz-criterion for $r > 0.5$.

This proposal of a general conception of rational behaviour in a continuum of situations of decision shows how it might be possible to avoid the aporia of the theory of rational decision in situations of uncertainty.

CHAPTER 6

# Non-consequentialist Economic Rationality

## 1. Two Kinds of Economic Rationality

Often it is assumed that there is basically only one kind of economic rationality. In fact there are at least two quite different kinds of economic rationality. One we might call the 'consequentialist', and the other the 'coherentist'. There might be more than just two different kinds of economic rationality, but it seems to me that these two kinds are the two paradigmatic ones, i. e. all other kinds of economic rationality are variants of one or the other. These two paradigmatic kinds of economic rationality are not kept separate because an identification of these two kinds would make the theory of economic rationality immune to almost every kind of critique, including the counterfactual critique.

Present-day economic theory does not presuppose universal egotism as it did during its early days. The legitimate heir of universal egotism is agent-centered consequentialism. The idea is roughly this: everybody has certain subjective goals. It is rational to optimize these goals. Therefore, it is rational to choose efficient means for reaching these goals. The rational action is an efficient means to reach one's subjective goals.

Philosophers usually use the term 'consequentialism' for characterizing a certain type of ethical theory. This type of ethical theory regards the Right as a trivial function of the Good.[1] Doing the right thing means optimizing the Good. Since morality is constituted from a universalist point of view, the ethical theory of the Good asserts that the Good is the same for everybody. The ideal moral world would be inhabited by agents, all maximizing the same subjective value function over the set of consequences of actions, and these interpersonally invariant value functions would represent the ranking in terms of 'morally better'. The most natural interpretation of this theory is the objectivist -

---

[1] Cf. Broome (1991).

like the theory of David Brink or Dieter Birnbacher -, but subjectivist interpretations of this account prevail also, like the theories of Richard M. Hare or Rainer Trapp.[2]

The emphasis on the one interpersonally invariant moral valuation of ethical consequentialism explains why philosophers and ethicists usually regard any weakening of the claim that there is only one common moral good for everybody as a departure from consequentialism - as do most prominently Thomas Nagel, Samuel Scheffler and Derek Parfit.[3] It is not worth arguing over terminology, but sometimes a certain form of terminology inhibits theoretical understanding. There is a common element in theories of practical rationality, namely the claim that it is rational to act such that the consequences of acting are optimal in terms of given subjective goals on the one hand, and ethical theories which tell that an act is morally right, if and only if its consequences maximize moral value, on the other: both accounts assume the same theory of the (rational or moral) Right. The Right is a simple function of the Good - the Right maximizes the Good. This common element can also be put in epistemological terms: if you know the causal and probabilistic consequences of an action, you know everything necessary to judge the action to be right or wrong.

The coherentist theory of economic rationality on the other hand imposes restrictions on individual preferences - restrictions like transitivity: if a person prefers A to B and B to C, she should prefer A to C.[4] The difference between the consequentialist and the coherentist account of economic rationality can also be explained in terms of motivation. The consequentialist account places restrictions on the kind of motivation a rational person should have (she should aim at optimizing the consequences of her actions), whereas the coherentist account does not deal with motivation at all, but does place restrictions with regard to certain structural traits of preferences. Described in this manner, there seems to be no reason at all to identify the consequentialist and the coherentist account of economic rationality. It would take a separate study to investigate how it came about that these two theories were identified with each other. The idea of introducing a notion of 'utility' meeting certain epistemological requirements, especially the

---

[2] See Brink (1989), Birnbacher (1988), Hare (1981) and Trapp (1988).

[3] See Nagel (1980), Scheffler (1982) and Parfit (1986).

[4] For a more technical exposition see ch. 2, sec.1.

requirement to be testable against empirical data, respectively observable behaviour, certainly played a central rôle.[5] Today those strict versions of empiricism are obsolete, but the confusion for which they were responsible in the theory of economic rationality still remains.

However, this confusion would not cause much damage if the consequentialist account of economic rationality were adequate, since it is certainly compatible with the coherentist account. The problem which we will be discussing in this chapter results from the fact that the consequentialist account of practical rationality is defective. Therefore, if economic rationality were identified with the consequentialist account, it would be at best a theory adequate for one specific kind of action, and the area of economic analysis would be unduely limited. A more promising strategy seems to be to strengthen the coherentist interpretation of economic rationality by confining the consequentialist interpretation to certain fields of application where this seems to be adequate, e. g. ideal market situations.

## 2. The Problem of Cooperation

The argument for a coherentist notion of economic rationality is relevant only if the standard consequentialist rationality is inadequate. Otherwise, the consequentialist understanding could be taken to be the natural interpretation of the postulates of the coherentist account. There are many arguments against consequentialism in ethics but also against consequentialism as a general theory of practical rationality. Among these there are not only traditional ethical arguments like the incompatibility of consequentialism and individual rights, as it was developed e. g. by Robert Nozick, or the incompatibility of integrity and consequentialism, or the relevance of normative institutions which cannot be made plausible by consequentialist ethics etc., but there are also arguments stemming from collective choice theory like the Gibbard-Satterthwaite theorem showing that consequentially optimizing agents can never reach stable results of collective decision making, and the Liberal Paradox showing that even minimal liberalism cannot be guaranteed if one postulates that the collective decision procedure

[5] See also Sen (1978).

should be Pareto-inclusive, which certainly is an assumption common to all consequentialist theories. It is impossible here to discuss all these aspects which together constitute a forceful critique of consequentialist notions of practical rationality and also of morality. Instead I will concentrate on one argument only, which I shall call the *argument from cooperation*, and it might remain open whether this argument is the basic one, i. e. whether all the other arguments are variants of this argument, or whether they can be reduced to the problem of cooperation.

As the first step, consequentialism in the theory of practical rationality has to be characterized as sufficiently clearcut in order to match the underlying intuitions. If a person does $x$ and $x$ belongs to a certain type of action $T$, then one might say in doing $x$ that as a consequence the person did something of type $T$. If 'consequences' of this kind are included, then optimizing the consequences could cover every theory of practical rationality, including those which we do not want to call consequentialist.

Take for example the Kantian theory of moral action. Indeed, with Kant the heart of morality is constituted by the assumption that humans are rational beings. As much as he is a rational being, his subjective motivating rules (*Maximen*) are subject to a test of rationality: the general application of these subjective rules must not lead to incoherence. Self-defeating is the most stringent variation of incoherence: subjective rules the general application of which is undesirable for the acting person are irrational, *a fortiori* those subjective rules the general application of which is logically impossible. This compatibility test of subjective rules marks three concentric areas of morality, respectively rationality: logical incompatibility constitutes that which is unconditionally wrong, which violates 'perfect duties'; voluntary incompatibility constitutes that which is conditionally wrong ('imperfect duties'); and the altruistic consideration of the desires of others constitutes the realm of the supererogative. What one ought to do is not determined by what consequences the considered action has in relation to other possible actions, but what would be the case if actions motivated like this would become a general practice. Both rule-utilitarianism and Kantian ethics do not allow to judge what is right by looking at the consequences of one's actions. This is an important difference to act utilitarianism which would be concealed by taking one property of actions as belonging to a certain type or being motivated by a certain attitude as part of the consequences of this action. Ideal rule-utilitarianism and Kantianism are certainly not consequentialist theories in so far as the criterion of the right is constituted by a fictitious test and not by the actual consequences. To pass this fictitious test is not the same as having actual consequences. If one chooses a terminology which allows to interpret every property of an action as a consequence of this action if it is done, the difference between fiction and reality or between a counterfactual test and actual consequences would be given up which is certainly unacceptable.

In a broader perspective think of actions as being of causal relevance for the course of history in the most general sense. In doing so we cause certain changes in the world. Consequentialism instructs us to look at these changes, and then to judge on the basis of some value function and to determine whether these changes are desirable. To exclude pseudo-consequences, one has to look at the consequences as independent from the respective action. They are not independent in the sense that they were not caused by the respective action, but rather independent in the sense that they can be valued without knowing which act caused them. In most general terms, we can discriminate between historic and unhistoric predicates for describing possible worlds. Only unhistoric predicates, predicates which can be applied without knowing the history of the world, are admitted for describing possible worlds or set of possible worlds as the consequences of actions.[6] For example, utilitarians agree that only one entity has intrinsic value, and this is individual well-being. Certainly the predicate 'aggregate individual well-being', applied to states of the world, is an unhistoric one. A more sophisticated version could include distributional aspects as well, without turning to historic predicates.

Normatively understood, the theory says that one ought to do $x$ if $x$ has optimizing consequences. There are then two cases: the first is where the value functions interpersonally differ (this is the general case). In the case of interpersonally varying value functions, there are interaction situations in which consequentially optimizing actions on the part of the participants lead to an outcome which is worse for everyone than if the participants had behaved differently. A well-known paradigm of such an interaction situation is that of the prisoners' dilemma. This type of interaction situation occurs frequently.

---

[6] See also ch. 7.

Neither the Axelrod results nor the theory developed by David Gauthier have shown that the conflict of individual optimization and collective optimality (Pareto-inclusiveness) vanishes if one considers iterated prisoner dilemma games or introduces dispositions from which to choose.[7]

It is plausible to assume that probably not in all, but in some genuine prisoners' dilemma cases, one ought to cooperate. At least if one does not regard external effects, then cooperation is advised by almost every ethical criterion which has been discussed in the history of philosophical ethics like the categorical imperative, rule utilititarianism, act utilitarianism, impartial observer theories, universal sympathy theories etc. Almost all ethical theories advise to cooperate if no external effects tell against it. It is utmost implausible to assume that cooperation in genuine prisoners' dilemma situations is always wrong, respectively that one must never cooperate in prisoners' dilemma situations. Rendering cooperation irrational in all cases is inadequate if the theory of rationality is to be understood normatively. Obviously, we sometimes have good reasons to act cooperatively, and in these cases - by definition of cooperation - we do not optimize individually.

Cooperation might be a very basic type of justification for an action which is not compatible with consequentialism, if one assumes interpersonally differing value functions, but it is certainly not the only one. Take, e. g., reasons for actions such as 'I promised to do *x*', which under ordinary conditions is a good reason to do *x*. Or perhaps, if you suddenly realize that you acted wrongly, you might have a good reason to apologize, etc. There is a vast variety of types of good *prima facie* reasons.[8] These types may be divided into moral and nonmoral ones, other-regarding and self-regarding ones, and consequential and nonconsequential ones. I personally think that this vast variety of good reasons can be reduced by introducing the notion of structural rationality, but this idea will not be developed here (cf. ch. 2, sec. 4). In any case, there can be no doubt that if we understand the normative theory of practical rationality as a theory of good reasons for actions, then rational actions in many cases do not have optimizing consequences. In fact there is only one way out for the consequentialist notion of practical rationality if it is understood normatively: one accepts only one

[7] See Axelrod (1984), Schüssler (1990), Gauthier (1986), and ch. 8 in this volume.
[8] See also ch. 9.

interpersonally invariant ranking of states of the world (consequences), i. e. one interpersonally invariant value function. As a theory of practical rationality, this assumption disregards the central rôle that personal projects, personal bindings and altruism, regarding near-by persons, bear upon rational action. Furthermore, we can exclude on the basis of many anthropological observations the hope that persons will form value functions which are even only approximately interpersonally invariant. This does not seem to be a sound assumption, and the normative theory of practical rationality should certainly not be based on such an illusionary project.

If we understand the theory of practical rationality as a basically empirical theory (characterizing an ideal type of behaviour under certain conditions), we arrive at the same result. Understood descriptively, the consequentialist theory of practical rationality is at odds with many empirical studies in game theory. Even in one-shot prisoners' dilemma games there is a high percentage of cooperative decisions as Anatol Rapoport's classical study has early shown.[9] Choosing the cooperative strategy means - by definition of the prisoners' dilemma - not to optimize the consequences of one's actions. But if preferences were revealed by choices, then 'cooperation' reveals preferences which are not in accord with the assumed structure of the prisoners' dilemma in the respective situation. In this way, what in fact is the choice of the cooperative strategy in a prisoners' dilemma *ipso facto* removes the prisoners' dilemma. This cannot be adequate, because without this underlying structure it does not make sense anymore to speak of cooperation. We conceptually exclude what we wanted to explain: cooperation. If we ask the agents about how they rank the possible consequences of actions, they might reveal a prisoners' dilemma structure and at the same time they might prefer cooperation to non-cooperation, which is not compatible with both consequentialist optimization and the assumption that the situation has a prisoners' dilemma structure. To define 'true' preferences by revealed preferences just begs the question as to whether the consequentialist account of economic rationality is adequate. The crucial test of every agent-centered consequentialist theory of practical rationality is how it deals with cooperation. If a theory of practical rationality rules out cooperative action by conceptual means, it illegitimately evades this

[9] Rapoport (1965).

test. If we want to conceptually allow for cooperative action, it is necessary to distinguish between the valuation of consequences and the ranking of actions. Ranking actions is not the same as ranking consequences of actions.

This last remark leads directly to the logical aspects of the theory of practical rationality. Logically understood, a theory of practical rationality connects different relevant concepts with each other - it develops a conceptual frame. This frame should be theoretically fruitfull, i. e., it should foster the development of good normative and/or descriptive theories and it should meet certain conditions of adequacy, since the notion of rationality is deeply intertwined with other central notions of our belief system. If, e. g., 'action' (or 'strategy') is defined as being a function from circumstances to consequences or being a probability distribution over the class of subsets of the set of possible worlds, then the valuation of a strategy is by itself a valuation of consequences or probability distributions, and this is inadequate if rational action is not to be just a trivial function of the value of its consequences, as consequentialism assumes. The difference between the consequentialist and the coherentist account of practical rationality can only be made explicit if the conceptual frame is compatible with some kind of differentiation between the question as to which consequences of actions are desirable and the question as to which strategy is rational, or to put it in more philosophical terms, between the theory of the Good and the theory of the Right.

## 3. The Rational and the Good

In general, the Good is agent-relative. Therefore, a society can be understood as a complex game-theoretic structure. If there was only one interpersonally invariant Good, then society would transform from a multi-person-supergame into a one-person supergame - a supergame in which there is only one kind of interaction: coordination. In such a society, there would be no genuine conflicts, there would be no prisoners' dilemmas nor chicken games etc., and even the difference between cooperative and non-cooperative games would cease to exist. The complexity of good reasons for action represents the game-theoretic complexity of social interaction. The Rational is not a simple consequentialist function of the Good. Rational agency is determined by both the values involved and the structure of the interaction. The defects of consequentialist rationality are the result of neglecting the rôle which structural traits of interaction have for the determination of rational action. Optimizing the consequences of one's actions can be called rational in the normative sense (i. e. can be prescribed) only under specific conditions. In the most general sense, these conditions are constituted by structural traits which are worth being preserved. If economic rationality were identified with agent-relative consequentialist rationality, then it would be adequate only under these specific conditions. Ideal market conditions are only one type of these conditions. If there are no external effects and those requirements which allow for communication and contracts being fulfilled, then situations are ruled out where individual optimization of consequences can have Pareto-inefficient results. The ideal market may be a morally free zone,[10] but it is dependent on, even more constituted by morality. The efficient market rests on normative structures - it presupposes that individual optimization is limited by constitutive rules of communication and cooperation. But if these constitutive rules are effective, then individual optimization can be recommended as rational under ideal market conditions. But in all cases of external effects, individual optimization alone cannot be the criterion of practical rationality. In these cases cooperative reasons enter the scene and a theory of practical rationality which does not take them into account is defective.

The economic theory of practical rationality faces, therefore, the following dilemma: it can adhere to the standard consequentialist account, but then it cannot claim to be normative (i. e. recommending, or prescribing), except in certain special cases like ideal market conditions; or it broadens its perspective by turning into a genuine coherentist account. There are advantages and disadvantages on both sides. The advantage of the first alternative is that it is closer to the specific notion of the 'economic man', originally an egoist, but now an agent-centered consequentialist.[11] The disadvantage of the first alternative is that it severely limits the field of application of economic analysis, whereas, on the contrary, the second alternative allows for the most general application of economic analysis, but at the same time cuts the

---

[10] See Gauthier (1986), ch. IV.

[11] Cf e. g. Edgeworth (1881) and Becker (1976).

last ties with psychological egoism. There are good justifications for each of these alternatives, but it is not possible, as a considerable part of economic analysis seems to assume, to have both: a theory of the 'homo oeconomicus' based on the most general and unconditioned account of practical rationality (coherence of preferences) and agent-centered consequentialism. Certainly, the utility theorem is misinterpreted if it is taken as a proof for the fact that at least one convincing version of a coherentist theory of practical rationality is equivalent to the consequentialist 'economic' rationality in the narrow sense.

The crucial point for a coherentist account of economic rationality is how the 'utility' function of this theorem can be interpreted. The theorem shows that the qualitative concept of preference can be transformed into a quantitative one (a real-valued function) if and only if certain conditions of coherence are met by these preferences. These conditions are certainly at odds with rational action in many cases, if the concept of action is identified with, e. g., lotteries over its consequences. In this case, cooperation (and since moral rules constitute a cooperation-problem: general conformity is better for everybody than gereral nonconformity, the following of moral rules in general) is not compatible with the dominance-criterion of rational choice, but the dominance-criterion is part of a convincing version of the coherentist theory of practical rationality. Accounts of bounded[12] and satisfycing[13] rationality violate, e. g., the monotony axiom, if the concept of action is introduced in such a way. The coherence conditions are adequate as minimal requirements for practical rationality only if structural traits of interaction are taken into account in order to determine the preference rankings of actions, i. e. more information than the one about consequences of actions and probabilities is needed. If these types of information are included, then there is no reason to assume that the ideally rational person would violate the coherence axioms. The transformation of a merely qualitative conceptual scheme into a quantitative scheme with two central concepts, the one of subjective probability and the one of subjective value, is again viable. However, subjective value in this sense is not the personal Good realized in certain states of the world which are caused by the person's actions. The Rational is not necessarily maximizing the Good anymore. Instead, this

---

[12] Simon (1983).

[13] Slote (1989).

value function represents the whole of the rational person's preferences, not merely the preferences regarding consequences of actions; this value function is well-defined if and only if these preferences are coherent - it represents coherent preferences. It is an open and difficult question as to how rich the conceptual means must be in order to describe these preferences adequately. Sometimes quite restricted information might suffice, e. g. information about consequences and their subjective probabilities - in these cases one can turn to the traditional narrow concept of (agent-centered and consequentialist) economic rationality. In other cases this is impossible, because then the analysis should be based on the broader coherentist account. This account of economic rationality, then, would not be consequentialist anymore.

CHAPTER 7

# Interpersonal Dependency of Preferences

## 1. Conditional Preferences

There are probably no unconditional preferences. Nevertheless it is useful to discriminate conceptually between conditional and unconditional, or categorical, preferences. A person's preference for $x$ over $y$ is *unconditional* if this preference is independent of the person's belief about the truth or falsity of any proposition $p$. If a person perferred $x$ to $y$ - prefers, e. g., eating vegetarian food to eating meat - but changed this preference after having been told that eating meat would improve her health, then she had a conditional preference. In this case the preference was not independent of any proposition.

In everyday life and in ordinary language, we have preferences for concrete actions in concrete circumstances: we prefer to do this rather than that; we have preferences for objects and states of affairs; we prefer certain cars to other cars; we prefer a just society to an unjust society etc.; many different entities can be objects of preferences.

All these objects of preference can be transformed into propositions - or rather we will assume this to be so. The transformation of a preference into a propositional preference requires a certain degree of expliciteness. 'I prefer European to American cars' might be transformed into 'I prefer to drive...' or 'I prefer to buy...' or 'I prefer to see ... on the roads.' These three transformations are obviously not equivalent. Propositional preferences should be presentable in a 'that'-clause. One should be able to express them by saying 'I prefer this to be the case rather than that to be the case;' 'I prefer that I buy...;' 'I prefer that I drive...;' 'I prefer that I see...'.

The propositions in the last paragraph were self-regarding. They had the form 'I prefer that I ...' But not all preferences are properly expressed by propositions that have this trait. I might prefer that *you* do something; or, I might prefer that something is the case without referring to myself as the preferring person. In everyday life and in ordinary language there are preferences which are not selfregarding. Preference theory cannot always account for these.

We must differentiate between cases in which the propositions (as the objects of preference) are *not self-regarding* on the one hand and cases that express a *certain type of conditional preference* on the other. Everyday preferences are all conditional preferences. But this is an empirical, contingent fact. Our everyday preferences are conditional because the objects of our preferences are elliptic. The objects we refer to name only certain elements or aspects of what we prefer. Since there is not enough time in everyday life to specify exactly what we prefer, expressing preferences is like giving hints. There is always some - factual or counterfactual - proposition which forces or would force us to change the preference.

In theory things look different. Decision theory - or at least its philosophical underpinning - tries to reduce the plurality of objects and motivations of preference to two kinds of propositional attitudes: desirability (utility) and belief (subjective probability).[1] This reduction is sometimes combined with the 'subjectivist standpoint' that only the actual and possible (or expected) subjective states of the acting person are, or should be relevant for her preferences. But this combination is not necessary and it is advisable to refrain from too strong 'metaphysical' presuppositions in the theory of practical rationality.

Our preferences which, in standard decision theoretic concepts, are supposed to be (directly) revealed by choice, i. e. by acting, are structured by objects of our desire. If we stick to the consequentialist interpretation as it is revealed in the usual modes of how to apply de-

---

[1] In Savage (1954), the subjectivist standpoint is even made explicit insofar as he identifies consequences with subjective states of the acting person (see Savage (1954), p. 14). For a philosophical exposition of a subjectivist *cum* consequentialist notion of practical rationality see Griffin (1986). According to the structuralist account in the philosophy of science (see e. g. Sneed (1971), Moulines (1976) and Stegmüller (1979b)) a scientific paradigm is characterized fundamentally by two components: a (mathematical) structure and a (paradigmatic) range of applications. Basic concepts are (partly) interpreted by specific examples of application. The paradigm of standard decision theory common to all models is subjectivist *cum* consequentialist in terms of standard applications (on 'paradigmatic' case-studies cf. e. g. Becker (1976)). For an analysis of different models of decision theory in terms of expliciteness and application see Spohn (1978); supplementary material is contained in Nida-Rümelin (1987a) and in Schmidt (1995).

cision-theoretic analysis, then the next step would be to analyze those characteristics of the respective situation (in which the preferences are revealed) which are responsible for those preferences. It might well be that reasonable and well-informed persons exhibit similar evaluative attitudes. It could even turn out that Savage's self-oriented consequentialism is adequate insofar as reasonable persons exhibit this type of evaluative attitudes. More probably, however, the inadequacy of this account would become quite obvious. Therefore, it is advisable to refrain from theoretical restrictions as far as it seems viable. One form of expressing this kind of theoretical asceticism is to leave the interpretation of outcomes (or consequences) open (an idea which led Jeffrey to his holistic propositional account of decision theory).[2] Nevertheless, it is not easy to get rid of consequentialism in interpreting and applying decision-theoretic models above all because of the identification of actions with lotteries. A lottery is a probability distribution over consequences. Consequences are usually supposed to be events or - more broadly speaking - propositions (not every proposition is an event). But how can a probability distribution over propositions (outcomes) induce an evaluative attitude and in turn a (revealed) preference, in case the acting person is not able to evaluate the possible outcomes regarding the lotteries (actions) in question, because she has a strict preference in favour of one proposition over another only if she can assume certain *ceteris paribus*-conditions. More broadly speaking: in general persons prefer one proposition to another not intrinsically but as the result of further practical considerations including probabilistic ones. These preferences on their turn are a legitimate object of a complete theory of practical rationality and it is reasonable to assume that the same criterion (maximize expected utility, MEU) should be applied here as well: an action is identified with a lottery; a lottery is a probability distribution over propositions (events); a proposition is a set of possible worlds; the evaluative ranking of a proposition depends on the probability distribution on the set of subsets of this set of possible worlds (every subset of a set of possible worlds is itself a proposition, at least we shall assume this for the sake of simplicity). This dependency is in accordance with the MEU-criterion. This kind of reduction ends in an evaluative ranking of possible worlds, more precisely the atomic propositions which are singletons of possible worlds.

[2] Jeffrey (1965a).

Every characteristic which could be relevant for the determination of our preferences can seemingly be taken into consideration if only the language in which possible worlds are described is rich enough.

We can therefore assume that a rational preference relation yields a complete ranking of possible worlds, hence the ordering axioms are conceptually linked to the concept of a rational preference. A rational preference relation constitutes (or results in) a complete ranking of possible worlds. On this account, preferences over actions are preferences over lotteries with the latter having possible worlds (respectively sets of possible worlds) as their outcomes. This is so since every action induces a specific probability distribution over the set of all sets of possible worlds as possible consequences of the action.

Thus, the phenomenom of conditional preferences seems to vanish: there are no conditional preferences any more since every conditionalization can be incorporated into the description of possible worlds as the new objects of preference. But this solution overlooks one special but important kind of conditional preferences: *interpersonally dependent preferences*.[3] They constitute an important kind of conditional preferences because (a) many preferences in our social world are *de facto* interpersonally dependent, (b) this interdependency of preferences is a characteristic trait of interacting *persons* as a version of second or higher order desires and volitions[4] and (c) this interpendency constitutes a problem not only in practice but also *in theory*. In this chapter, I shall argue for the claim (c).

---

[3] To my knowledge, Frederic Schick first brought up the problem of interdependent preferences in the context of collective choice theory, but his critique did not initiate a fundamental revision of preference theory. In his paper 'Democracy and Interdependent Preferences' (Schick (1972)), he proposed two new procedures for aggregating preferences, one is a version of the ranking method, the other relies on the identification of an optimal attainable equilibrium (cf. also Schick (1971)). Certainly, both methods allow for a much more refined analysis of collective choice procedures compared to the usual ones in Arrow's conceptual frame (cf. Arrow (1951)), but if my argument is sound, new procedures of aggregation based on a uniform concept of preference do not really solve the problem. I shall not discuss how the concept of preference has to be modified in order to allow for an adequate treatment of interdependent preferences. One possibility is to use the concept of a social position, which, e. g., allows to make the concept of categorical preferences more explicit, cf. Kern/Nida-Rümelin (1994) ch. 8 and 11.

[4] Cf. Frankfurt (1971); Dennett, 'Conditions of Personhood', in Dennett (1978).

## 2. Interpersonally Dependent Preferences

Most kinds of conditional preferences can be *deconditionalized* by the model sketched in the first section. Most propositions can be incorporated into a new description of the set of alternatives as the objects of preference. In theory, this incorporation ends up in the set of possible worlds.

Not all propositions responsible for changes in preference can be thus incorporated. All propositions which are not about the description of possible worlds or states of affairs are excluded. Which propositions can be made part of the description of possible worlds depends on the *mode of description*. This depends on the predicates admitted.

We should distinguish between *historic* and *unhistoric predicates*. Unhistoric predicates can be applied to a possible world without knowing its historic context. Unhistoric predicates suffice to describe a state of the world in the literal sense. A state of the world is realized at one specific point in time. In principle, it can be described totally without reference to history. With the help of this, the difference between consequentialist notions of practical rationality and non-consequentialist ones can be made explicit: if it suffices to know the probability distribution induced by a certain action over the set of possible worlds described with unhistoric predicates alone to decide whether the action is rational, then the theory is consequentialist; otherwise it is non-consequentialist. Non-consequentialist rationality is characterized by conditional preferences in which the conditioning propositions cannot be incorporated in a description of possible worlds by means of unhistoric predicates alone. Several chapters contain arguments establishing that consequentialist notions of practical rationality are defective. Yet for the sake of the argument here we can confine the analysis to a consequentialist notion of practical rationality. *Even if one adheres to consequentialism, and even if one is interested only in the abstract model of rational preferences, there remains the problem of conditional preferences.*

This problem is engendered by a *specific kind* of conditionalization: its conditioning propositions are *other persons' preferences*. One can think that ideally a rational person's ranking of possible worlds is fully determined by complete knowledge concerning both the full description of these worlds and the probabilities the action induces. Letting probabilities aside, the ranking is determined by the full description of alternative states of the world. Every consequentialist conditionalization can be incorporated into the description. If my ranking is conditioned by another person's preferences, this can be incorporated as well. But consider a case in which not only my preferences are conditioned by this person's preferences, but also this person's preferences are conditioned by my preferences. Now, the preferences are underdetermined, for both rankings cannot be determined at once. Even without giving up consequentialism, the deconditionalization of preference turns out to be impossible.

*Interdependency leads to underdetermination.* If preferences are interdependent they cannot be deconditionalized even in theory. Certainly, in practice, limited knowledge might help. Persons with interdependent preferences guess the other persons' preferences and thus fix their rankings. But this solution is defective. These rankings are sensitive to information. In the general case, every person out of a group with interdependent preferences has to change her ranking whenever she knows about the other persons' actual preferences. At least in theory it should be possible to fix the individual rankings of possible worlds under the condition of complete knowledge. If an $n$-tupel of individual rankings of $n$ persons with interdependent preferences is not sensitive to revelation we say that it is in *equilibrium*.

In game theory, the preference rankings over outcomes (possible worlds) are fixed and the equilibrium is an equilibrium of (pure or randomized) strategies.[5] Here, the equilibrium is an equilibrium of preferences or subjective valuations. Since, according to the standard interpretation of decision theory, practical rationality is defined in terms of given preferences over outcomes or possible worlds, we cannot talk about preferences in equilibrium as rational preferences: there are no preferences anymore on which the notion of rationality can be based.

Even if interdependent preferences in equilibrium cannot be called rational in the usual decision theoretic sense, they might be regarded as the plausible result of empathy - be it sympathy or aversion. Examples make it plausible that even *if* there is an equilibrium, this can generally

---

[5] For a critical discussion and game-theoretic criteria of rational choice, esp. the notion of equilibrium cf. W. Spohn, 'Wie läßt sich Spieltheorie verstehen?', in Nida-Rümelin (1994c).

not be interpreted as a combination of plausible preferences given certain interdependencies.[6] But even without this point, the problem of underdetermination would persist, since in most cases there is no equilibrium point, as a mathematical result I shall present in the next section shows.

### 3. The Two-Person-Case

In order to formalize the problem of underdetermination, let us consider the case of two persons, A and B. Classical expected utility theory does not provide any technical tools which might help in representing the interdependent preferences by a cardinal utility function. However, we assume that such a representation is possible and that we therefore are now able to work with real-valued bounded utility functions.[7] Thus, without loss of generality, we can assume the functions to have values in the unit interval (between 0 and 1). In the non-interdependent case, A and B can be seen as assigning real numbers $a$ and $b$ to each state, respectively. In the interdependent case, however, the value a person can be seen to assign to a state also depends upon the value the other person assigns to that state and vice versa. Suppose now, that A and B find themselves facing a state they wish to evaluate and that their preferences are interdependent. Initially, neither person knows the value the other person assigns to the state and is, therefore, assumed to

---

[6] Cf. Nida-Rümelin (1987a), ch. 7.

[7] Facing the general practise of using cardinal utility functions even when the utility is not arrived at by constrained preferences, this does not seem to be too strong a heuristic assumption in this context. See, e. g., the discussion of different criteria for decision situations under uncertainty in Luce/Raiffa (1957), pp. 275 ff. However, although I cannot give a full formal treatment in this chapter, I believe it to be possible to cardinalize interdependent preferences using a modification of the classical axiomatics, e. g. the one in Luce/Raiffa (1957), pp. 24 ff, along the following lines. Take as alternatives first of all a set of states, where two different states are regarded as equal if they merely differ in a person's preference. Then differenciate this set of states by adding to the descriptions phrases such as '... and the value P assigns to it is $x$.' With this set, form gambles in the usual fashion and constrain a person's preferences over this extended set by the standard coherence axioms. Of course, this only leads to a class of utility functions which can be narrowed down, for our purposes, by linear transformation to functions bounded by 0 and 1.

estimate the valuation. Based on this first estimation, the two persons are able to give a valuation of the state. An exchange of the information about this valuation leads to a second basis for individual evaluation and so forth.

Note that the model is only designed to represent situations of a very special kind. Typically, interdependent preferences are dependent on certain facts about the world and on facts about the other person's preference. Formalizing these kinds of preferences is mathematically relatively complicated. Even more so is the attempt to gain formal results within such a framework. Therefore, we confine us to the evaluation of only one state, and the preference (resp. the utility) is not dependent on which state actually obtains but only on the other person's evaluation of the very same state and an interdependency function corresponding to subjective utility in the classical model. In classical utility theory, there would be only one utility value associated with this state. In the notion under discussion here, this single value cannot be assumed, since what also matters are the utilities of the other person. The result presented below shows that even in this very simplified case the valuations generally cannot be expected to converge. This is why I believe that this makes it more than plausible that very much the same problem occurs in situations of a more complex type in which states are not only differentiated by persons' valuations but also by propositions describing the world.

We are now in the position to express the model in a more mathematical language. In the case of two persons and one state we can take the persons to 'have' valuation functions $f$ (person A) and $g$ (person B), such that the value person A assigns to state $z$ does depend on the value person B assigns to $z$ and vice versa. Assume $y_0$ and $x_0$ to be the first guesses A and B make of each others valuations, respectively. This leads to a first announcement of individual valuations, namely $f(y_0)$ for A and $g(x_0)$ for B. This is taken as a basis for a second valuation, which is $f(g(x_0))$ for A and $g(f(y_0))$ for B, which, again, serves as a basis for a further valuation and so on. We have, thus, recursively defined two sequences generated by the initial values $x_0$, $y_0$ and the valuation functions $f$ and $g$. The crucial question is whether these converge. If they do not converge, there is no fixed value which a person can be taken to assign to the state. We assume the functions to be increasing or decreasing. I. e., either a person's valuation increases with the valuation of another person (pro-attitude), or the valuation decreases with the valuation of the other person (con-attitude) or - in the case of indifference - the valuation is constant.

Suppose Harry and Sally have decided a couple of days ago to meet in a pub tonight. They meet at 8 PM and go straight to the pub. After having settled down there they simultaneously ask each other the question 'How do you like the music here?' to begin a conversation. We assume their utility functions ($f$ for Harry and $g$ for Sally) to be interdependent and hence, in order to answer the question, they have to estimate the utility ('ranking of the quality of the music') of the other person, respectively. This leads to the initial values $x_o$ (Sally's estimation of Harry's value) and $y_o$ (Harry's estimation of Sally's value), and to the announcement of their first approximation $f(y_o)$ (Harry) and $g(x_o)$ (Sally). Hereafter, they take these new values as basis for a second announcement, namely $f(g(x_o))$ (Harry) and $g(f(y_o))$ (Sally). And so on. Clearly, the 'classical case' without interdependency is representable in our model by constant utility functions $f$ and $g$. What used to be a fixed utility value assigned to a state, now becomes a function in which this utility is not constant but varies with the value the other person assigns to the state. We take it that the monotony we assumed above is an implication of rationality. While in the classical case the other person's utility does not affect the valuation of the first one, in our model this can be the case. But, obviously, interdependency means that the constancy of utilities is changed by the person intrinsically wanting the other person to assign more (in the case of a pro-attitude) or less (in the case of a con-attitude) value to the state in question. If there is a function which is increasing on a certain interval and decreasing on another, then the person with this function does not seem to have formed a clear attitude towards the other, and it is unclear as to how one could rationally arrive at such a function.

Without pursuing the mathematical details here, I state the result which a concise mathematical analysis of the model yields.[8] It can be shown that even if there is a given case of convergence, a tiny change either in the initial values or in the shape of the valuation functions leads to divergence. To put this fact in a slightly more mathematical language: with respect to the usual topology on the real numbers, the set of cases for which the sequences diverge is dense in the set of all cases. Of course, this does not necessarily mean that there are more

[8] For a mathematical treatment see Nida-Rümelin/Schmidt/Munk (1996).

divergent than convergent cases. Nevertheless, this result questions very much the notion of well-determined subjective valuations in the case of interdependent uniform preferences.

## 4. Interpretation

Facing a situation of interdependent preferences (or: utilities) which the above model tries to represent[9], the question arises in what sense, if there is such a sense at all, one can still maintain a notion of 'individual preference' (resp. 'subjective utility'). As I noted above, the model and the mathematical treatment is restricted to a very special kind of interdependency and to a specific kind of iteration. The claim connected with these restrictions is, that despite of this possible lack of generality of the model, the fact that radical indeterminacy of whether convergence can be expected cuts down expectations for more complicated cases as well. However, even if we have a case in which the iterated valuations do converge, it still is not clear as to whether at all the limits of the two sequences can be regarded as plausible candidates for individual utilities upon which a normative theory could be based. This rather negative point follows from the Harry&Sally-example given above. There, independently of the starting estimations, both valuations can converge to zero. However, if we change Harry's valuation function and leave Sally's constant, it may well be the case that both do not converge to zero for any initial pair of valuations. What might be taken to be subjective utilities (namely the limits of the iterated valuations) are, therefore, relative to the situation in which the person finds herself (in our model relative to the other person's valuation function and possibly also to the initial valuations). This fact seems to undermine the solidity of a concept which provides only one uniform value function based on subjective preferences.

---

[9] The model used here is extremely simple. But it suffices to see that the answer which one might try, namely to save the uniform value function based on revealed subjective preferences, which is to regard equilibrium states of interdependent valuations as the real utilities, would be inadequate. There are relations to the theory of dynamical games, see e. g. Holler/Illing (1993, pp. 113 ff.) and Skyrms (1992), which can not be discussed here.

CHAPTER 8

# Practical Reason and Metapreferences

## 1. Rational Preference

An essential part of economic analysis is based on the description of individual preferences. The highly advanced mathematical theory used in economic analysis can handle individual preferences even in complex interaction situations. The basic theorem underlying this mathematical theory is that a person's preferences can be represented as a numerical function (a 'subjective valuation function'), provided that a group of seemingly harmless rationality criteria are met by those preferences. This numerical representation of preferences constitutes what is usually referred to as 'utility theory'. The theory seems tautological: if a person prefers alternative $x$ to alternative $y$, then $x$ is assigned a higher value in the person's subjective valuation function than $y$. However, as we will see, this tautological impression is unfounded.

For our purpose it is irrelevant on which kind of axiomatic characterizations the utility function is based, because our thesis that rational choice of action in general cannot be construed as some kind of maximizing preference fulfillment, is dependent only on the dominance principle, which is a common feature of all versions of utility theory given only that the probabilities of the relevant circumstances are independent from which action is chosen. My critique should not be understood as a refusal of some set of conditions for rational preference relations (which via metrification allow for attributing utility functions) but as an argument against the usual consequentialist interpretation of utility theory and the philosophy of action behind it. In fact it is possible to accept the von Neumann/Morgenstern axioms as an adequate characterization of a rational preference relation and simultaneously reject the consequentialist view that rational action maximizes preference fulfillment. But it is not within the scope of this chapter to show what implication a non-consequentialist interpretation would have for the decision theoretic model of rational choice.

## 2. The Problem of Cooperation

In some situations of interaction, individual rational behaviour on the part of the participants leads to an outcome which is worse for everyone than if the participants had behaved otherwise. Especially interesting are those situations where this predicament cannot be resolved by providing the participants with more information. A well-known and simple example of such a situation is the 2x2-prisoners' dilemma (PD).

If one of the prisoners (*B*) confesses, then it is in the other prisoner's (*A*) interest to confess as well. If *B* does not confess, then it is nevertheless in *A*'s interest to confess, because then *A* will be let off free as supergrass witness. The same reasoning is true for *B*, i. e., completely irrespective of what the other prisoner does, it is always in the interest of each to confess. It can be assumed that, under normal circumstances, confessing maximizes each of the prisoners' subjective valuation functions (which are not necessarily identical with their respective utility functions). Therefore, they both confess and each receives, say, a five-year prison sentence, although had they both remained silent, each could have come away with only, say, a one-year sentence.

While they are both sitting out their five-year prison terms, they never stop hearing from their wives that they have obviously behaved like idiots - rationally they should have kept their mouths shut. The classical economic theory of rationality, however, defends their behaviour as rational. Since this might count as some counter-intuitive feature of economic rationality, contemporary theorists have not been satisfied with this analysis and have tried to find ways in which the criminals could be freed from the accusation of irrational behaviour had they remained silent.[1] We want to show that at least the most prominent of these attempts to save the maximizing preference-fulfillment approach to rationality fails.

For the sake of simplicity we refer to the original PD example in the following discussion, but we require that the reader ignores, in a certain sense, the moral issues of the particulars in the situation: e. g., that it may be the duty of the prisoners to tell the truth, that punishment should be given to fit the crime, that measures are required for

[1] Cf. Axelrod (1981, 1984), Elster (1979, 1983), Opp (1983), Voss (1985), Kliemt (1985, 1986b).

the prevention of further misdeeds, etc. - these issues are not relevant to our analysis.

Let us assume that the prisoners decide to remain silent (they both decide to follow the cooperative strategy). We will consider this state of affairs as requiring an explanation. Both prisoners have apparently not behaved according to the maximization principle (in the sense of minimizing their prison terms). Yet, the apparently 'irrational' behaviour is advantageous because the outcome reached is better for each prisoner than that outcome they would have reached had they maximized their expected payoffs.

We distinguish four different types of solution models which attempt to explain this behaviour.

*Type 1 (The Irrationality Solution)*
The (cooperative) behaviour is explained by such things as the participants' lack of knowledge of the actual consequences of the alternatives, the minor intelligence of participants which prevents them from understanding the structure of the situation, the spontaneity of the participants' decisions, etc.; in short, by information deficits, epistemological irrationality, or inconsistency of the subjective valuation.

*Type 2 (The Shaftesbury Solution)*
The (cooperative) decision behaviour is explained by the fact that apart from egoistic motives (to spend as little time behind bars as possible), there are also altruistic motives, not to cause the other person too much harm, and similar considerations which contribute to decision behaviour.

*Type 3 (The Hobbesian Solution)*
One assumes that there are sanctions in society which prevent the criminal from confessing. The crinimal would have to expect, e. g., certain consequences from the world of organized crime if he acts as chief witness in the other criminal's prosecution.

*Type 4 (The Kantian Solution)*
The persons base their behaviour on collective rationality or in a more Kantian formulation: they act in such a way that they can wish that the maxim of their action can be made a general law within the 'small

world' of the prisoners. In this case, only cooperative behaviour, and not uncooperative behaviour fulfills the criterion.

The first type is theoretically relatively uninteresting. Of course, there may be many forms of irrationality, and it may even be the case that most decisions in everyday experience, with respect to an idealizing theory of rationality, would be characterized as irrational. Personally, I do not believe this to be true, but this is not at issue here. The first solution is not of theoretical interest because it would be enough to find one PD situation in which *rational* persons behave cooperatively[2] - in that situation this solution would fail and thus our conception of rationality would still be challenged.

There is a special commonality between explanation type 2 and type 3. While type 1 and type 4 do not challenge the fact that the interaction situation of the prisoners has a PD structure, for types 2 and 3 the situation is, in fact, not a PD situation.

I claim that the cooperation problem constitutes the central issue of social science. In the social and political sciences, explanation type 3 (Hobbes) dominates, in economics, explanation type 2 (Shaftesbury), in social psychology, explanation type 1, and in ethics, explanation type 4 (Kant). Advocates of these various types of explanation sometimes show a 'colonialistic attitude' towards their rivals; that is, they deny the legitimacy of all claims to promote any explanation other than their own. This led to many controversies between sociologists and psychologists, political theorists and sociologists, ethicists and sociologists, etc. Each of the six logically possible controversies has been present in some form.

The competing claims of explanations type 2 (Shaftesbury) and type 4 (Kant) are of special interest for the following reason: no one disputes that there is irrationality and that in many cases cooperative behaviour results from lack of information, poor consideration, or acting out of habit. No one disputes, either, that in many cases there are

---

[2] If we test an ideal type of practical rationality (PR), it is not enough to show that under assumptions of unlimited repetition and a certain correlatedness PR-rational persons would cooperate in PD-situations. To reject PR it suffices to show that there is one situation in which rational persons could choose act *a*, whereas this decision is irrational in terms of PR. Therefore it is not necessary for our argument to discuss Axelrod's interesting results for iterated PD games in this context.

legal sanctions and sanctions which arise out of everyday moral sensitivities which induce people to avoid uncooperative behaviour. But if there is some cooperative behaviour that cannot plausibly be explained by these two types of explanations - irrationality (type 1) or sanctions (type 3) - we must ask which of the remaining alternatives can provide an adequate explanation. Therefore the original thesis of this chapter, that a critique of decisions is not necessarily a critique of preferences takes a new form: in many cases type 2 is an adequate explanation of those other cases, but not in all - ethics should concentrate on the analysis of the Kantian type of cooperative behaviour.

A persons's subjective interests are not always in agreement with what that person considers to be his 'duty' - what he feels he should do. Furthermore, actual individual decision behaviour often deviates from what a person considers 'right' or 'advisible' (this has been discussed using the term 'akrasia' ever since Aristotle's Nicomachean Ethics). But on the other hand, indidvidual decision behaviour is not completely determined by subjective interests. Therefore, we need to distinguish at least between preferences which represent the person's (subjective) interests and preferences representing the person's (subjective) moral judgements. Then we have to assume at least a third concept of preference: 'resulting' preferences, which rank state of affairs taking all (subjective) aspects into consideration. One may think of some kind of aggregate intrapersonal criterion, which resembles collective choice rules applied to different preference relations (i. e. 'moral' and 'interest' preferences). If we talk of preferences without any further qualification then we think of ranking state of affairs, not of ranking actions.

## 3. Moral Improvement

Maximizing behaviour in the sense we have established in section 1 has put the prisoners behind bars for five years (instead of one). Now there are two possibilities to save them from this fate (assuming that the prisoners are rational): to claim that rationally they should not maximize, or to claim that (rational) cooperation is maximizing.

The economic model of rationality would have to show that the second possibility exists. The most interesting of these attempts is undertaken using the concept of metapreferences, originally introduced by A. K. Sen.[3] Sen proposes new preference orderings to guarantee the cooperative solution.

*(1) The Assurance Game*

In the assurance game (AG) it is assumed that the prisoners have the following preferences regarding the four possible outcomes:

A: [C,C], [D,C], [D,D], [C,D]
B: [C,C], [C,D], [D,D], [D,C][4]

As long as the other prisoner behaves cooperatively, it is likewise preferred by each individual to behave cooperatively. If the other person does not behave cooperatively, then each individual prefers not to behave cooperatively. The condition on which the realization of the cooperative collective outcome [C,C] depends is the *mutual assurance* that the other person will behave cooperatively.

For comparison, the preferences in the PD are:

A: [D,C], [C,C], [D,D], [C,D]
B: [C,D], [C,C], [D,D], [D,C]

The PD preferences, as we have shown, lead to the outcome [D,D]. In the assurance game, in contrast to the PD, there are two equilibrium outcomes: [C,C] and [D,D]. But because the individual decision depends on what is expected of the other, it is in no way guaranteed that a collective equilibrium outcome will be reached. Only when the participants have the same subjective expectations of the other's decision, an equilibrium outcome does result. A fundamental feature of this game is that a cooperative outcome can be reached through an agreement which would not require external sanctions (in contrast to the PD).

---

[3] Sen's idea must be seen in the broader context of widening the economic paradigm of rationality - for similar proposals see for example H. G. Frankfurt (1971), Jeffrey (1974), T. C. Schelling (1978, 1980, 1984), A. O. Hirschmann (1982, 66-71), M. S. McPherson (1982), D. George (1984), W. Raub/T. Voss (1986, 1988).

[4] [C,D] denotes: prisoner *A* chooses the cooperative strategy (not confessing) and prisoner *B* chooses the non-cooperative strategy (confessing) - '*D*' refers to defection.

*(2) The Other Regarding Game (OR)*
The prisoners are assumed to have the following preferences regarding the four possible outcomes:

A: [C,C], [C,D], [D,C], [D,D]
B: [C,C], [D,C], [C,D], [D,D]

No matter how the other person behaves, each person prefers to behave cooperatively [C,C]. The cooperative outcome is in this case the dominant solution whereas in the PD the dominant solution is the non-cooperative outcome.

In the assurance game the collectively best outcome, the collectively rational decision, is reached when there exists mutual assurance of the other's willingness to cooperate. There would be no reason for the participants to act contrary to any treaty or agreement as to their intended actions, because the preferences are arranged such that players prefer the cooperative solution to any alternative. If there is mutual assurance of the other's willingness to cooperate, the collective decision [C,C] is not only rational with respect to AG preferences but also with respect to PD preferences. Thus, if the prisoners were to behave as if they had AG preferences and were to act on the assumption of a mutual willingness to cooperate, they would reach the rational collective outcome of the PD; whereas they reach the irrational collective outcome when they base their behaviour on PD preferences.

In the 'other regarding' game, on the other hand, the mutual assurance condition for cooperation is not necessary. In this game, the cooperative collective outcome [C,C] is dominant. This solution is, furthermore, collectively rational both with respect to AG preferences and PD preferences. The prisoners would thus be better off if they were to behave as if they had AG preferences.

With respect to AG and OR preferences, the collective outcome [C,C] is the best outcome for each prisoner. Although [C,C] is not the best outcome for the individual with respect to PD preferences, it is a better outcome for the individual than the one which would have been reached had the players followed their PD preferences. AG preferences guarantee the collective rational outcome with respect to PD preferences (which is also collectively rational with respect to AG and OR preferences) under the epistemological condition that there exists mutual assurance of cooperative behaviour, and AG preferences guarantee the collectively rational outcome even without any epistemological condition.

Thus, there are interaction situations in which individual rational behaviour leads to a collectively rational outcome when the individual rational behaviour is determined based on preferences other than those which actually constitute the situation. Does it therefore make sense to determine a moral ordering of preferences and to secure collective rationality by maximizing behaviour relative to these preferences? If the answer is 'yes' then the OR preferences would be ranked above the AG preferences, and the AG preferences would be ranked above the PD preferences.

Sen argues for metapreferences in the sense of a moral ordering of the possible individual preference orderings. Whereas the individual preference orderings are defined over the set of possible outcomes, the moral ordering is defined over the set of possible individual preference orderings. The interpretation of this moral preference ordering is, however, obscure. It is essential to recognize that there are three possible ways of understanding moral metapreferences which must be carefully distinguished:

(1) Moral metapreferences can be interpreted as advising the prisoners to behave *as if* they had certain preferences, even though they actually do not have those preferences.
(2) Moral metapreferences can be interpreted as advising the prisoners to have certain preferences, which should guide their behaviour.
(3) Moral metapreferences can be understood as constituting purely a moral evaluation of outcomes on the basis of given preferences.

In all three interpretations difficulties arise when one analyzes the situation thoroughly. Let us begin with the first case.

*ad (1)*

Based on the actual preferences in the situation, there is moral behaviour which is not the result of rational individual maximization (relative to the actual preferences), but which can be defined as the result of maximizing behaviour relative to an as-if preference relation. Because there are better and worse preference relations among these as-if preference relations, there is a metapreference relation which ranks the individual preference relations.

Can these as-if preferences be called moral preferences? Undoubtedly, it is the outcomes - given a certain preference structure and a certain interaction situation (here it is the prisoners' dilemma) - which are morally evaluated. The as-if preferences are evaluated based on how well and to what extent they secure the morally recommended outcome. This does not establish that the as-if preferences themselves are made up of moral evaluations. But if these as-if preference orderings were based on moral criteria we would have three levels for moral evaluation:

(1) Outcomes.
(2) Individual behaviour (individual contribution to the outcome).
(3) Individual preference relations defined over the outcomes (these are brought into a moral ordering by moral metapreferences).

What could be the rationale for moral evaluation connecting these three levels? In the case of the prisoners' dilemma, the moral evaluation of the consequences is simple: the cooperative collective outcome is (according to the Pareto criterion) better than the non-cooperative collective outcome (level 1). The conclusion that the individual cooperative behaviour is better than the individual non-cooperative behaviour (level 2) does not, however, necessarily follow, because it depends on the moral evaluation of the asymmetric collective outcomes. If the asymmetric collective outcome is ordered below the non-cooperative collective outcome (by the subjective moral judgements) then it is not clear how the individual behaviour should be morally evaluated. Depending on the probability $p$ that the other will behave cooperatively, $p(C)$, the person could justify $C > D$ (when $p$ is close to 1) and $D > C$ (when $p$ is close to 0).

Assuming that once we have a moral evaluation of level 1 it is possible to deduce a moral evaluation of level 2, but still we have to establish the third step: the moral metapreference scheme which brings the individual preference orderings into a moral ordering based on a moral evaluation of the indiviudual decisions. At this level of analysis the moral philosopher would be quite content if there was only a very rudimentary moral metapreference relation available, hailing perhaps only one of the individual preference orderings as morally correct and determining all the rest as morally forbidden.[5]

Apart from the interpretation problem of the preference relations which are supposed to be brought into a ranking by metapreferences - we are dealing here apparantly not with actual but with fictitious preferences - the question arises as to what is the basis for evaluation in the metapreference relation; the moral evaluation of consequences or the moral evaluation of individual behaviour. The usual interpretation is undoubtedly that the evaluation of (1) leads to (2) and (via game theory) evaluation of (2) leads to (3). Below (in section 3) we will see that this path for evaluating moral behaviour is not valid.

*ad (2)*

This second attempt to secure collective rationality by maximizing new types of preferences fails from the beginning as the following considerations show.

An interaction situation with *n* participants is defined by the set of individual (pure) strategies and the utility which the participants receive from the corresponding strategy combinations (the endpoints of the game tree in extensive form). For the sake of simplicity we assume that the characteristics of the outcomes are fully determined by the strategy combinations. Changes in the subjective preferences imply a constitutive change of the interactions situation itself. The prisoners' dilemma is defined by a certain subjective evaluation of the collective outcomes:

A: [D,C] > [C,C] > [D,D] > [C,D]
B: [C,D] > [C,C] > [D,D] > [D,C]

[5] The great incompleteness of this metapreference relation - from a group of 10 preference orderings of a person there are 45 ordered pairs and only 9 of these are elements of the metapreference relation - should not be eliminated by the assumption that one is indifferent between two morally forbidden preference relations. Such an assumption would exclude the possibility of gaining more refined moral understanding which would allow for a differentiation between more and less immoral options.

Other preferences determine a different subjective evaluation of the corresponding collective outcomes:
OR preferences:

A: [C,C] > [C,D] > [D,C] > [D,D]
B: [C,C] > [D,C] > [C,D] > [D,D]

AG preferences:

A: [C,C] > [D,C] > [C,D] > [D,D]
B: [C,C] > [C,D] > [D,C] > [D,C]

If the prisoners behave maximizing relative to these preferences, there is another - epistemic - cooperation problem in the case of AG preferences and no cooperation problem at all in the case of OR preferences.

So either the cooperation problem vanishes as a result of modified subjective preferences or the cooperation problem remains unsolved. It can easily be shown that the cooperation problem vanishes in all cases only when there is a very special case of interpersonal dependency of preferences which implies a utilitarian kind of subjective preferences.[6]

But if one is not content with this utilitarian solution, the cooperation problem remains and this would make a theory of practical reason indispensible.

*ad (3)*
Now we come to the third possibility - the normative metapreference theory as a theory of *second-order preferences*. The interpretation is based on the assumption that there are different kinds of preferences and that it is acceptable to ascribe different kinds of preferences to one single person in a given situation. Within this framework, it is possible to define the interaction structure by exclusive reference to the prisoners' subjective interests. Under this interpretation, the moral metapreference relation ranks either the prisoners' resulting preference relations or their subjective moral preferences. In both cases, the evaluation is based on the given *structure of subjective interests* (together with certain normative criteria or 'rules of aggregation').

---

[6] Cf. J. C. Harsanyi (1953, 1955, 1977a, 1977b, 1979, 1980).

The *interaction structure of the subjective interests* is - in analogy to the normal form of a game in game theory - determined by the number of players, their possible strategies, and their subjective interest function over the set of outcomes of the game. It is compatible with this interest-interpretation of the PD structure that a prisoner might consider the cooperative collective outcome [D,D] to be morally superior, he might even consider it superior in the sense of his resulting preferences. The moral metapreference relation may evaluate subjective moral preferences as well as resulting preferences, since resulting preferences can be morally better or worse just like subjective moral preferences (the subjective morality of Nazi leaders, e. g., was in general quite a bad morality). Typical questions relevant to the subjective moral preference relation are: which distribution of goods (determined by various collective decisions) is just? What is a fair interest compromise in the interaction situation? etc.

So this third interpretation is obviously twofold: we can consider the metapreference approach as (1) a possibility of evaluating *resulting* preferences, which via maximizing preference fulfillment guide the actual behaviour of economically rational persons, or (2) as a criterion for the *moral judgements* of the prisoners, which are represented in their subjective moral preference relation.

With a more thorough analysis of different preference structures, the inadequacy of the metapreference solution to the cooperation problem becomes clear (for all interpretations of the metapreference approach).

## 4. Types of Metapreferences in the Cooperation Dilemma

The prisoners' dilemma is an interaction situation with two persons, each with two corresponding strategy possibilities, and thus four collective decisions: [D,D], [C,D], [D,C], [C,C]. We assume that the consequences, which are relevant for the individuals' subjective valuations, are unambiguously determined by the strategy combinations (collective decisions). Each individual has 4! = 24 possibilities for ranking the four collective decisions. Altogether there are 24 x 24 = 576 possible individual preference ordering combinations. Since every prisoner has at least three kinds of preference relations - preferences based on personal interests, preferences based on subjective moral evaluations, and resulting preferences - there are 576 possible preference structures in a given 2 x 2-situation. We can assume that a large part of these preference structures does not actually arise due to psychological regularities. But analyzing all the rest of the preference structures would provide us with an agenda that could occupy us for years. We will therefore limit our concrete analysis for the present to some of the interesting particular cases.

If we require symmetry, the number of logical possible preference structures of one type is reduced from 579 to 24. If both prisoners have a resulting preference for outcome $x$ over outcome $y$ when both prisoners have an interest in realizing $x$ instead of $y$, then the number of possible preference structures is reduced further from 24 to 12.

This last condition is intuitively a very reasonable general interference rationality criterion:

$$\forall j \in K: \left[\forall i \in K: \langle x, x' \rangle \in Rw_i \rightarrow \langle x, x' \rangle \in Rres_i\right],$$

with $K$: set of participants, $Rw$: preference relation representing subjective interests, $R$res: resulting preference relation. We call the criterion the 'PRW' (**P**areto inclusiveness of individual **R**esulting preferences with respect to individual **W**elfare preferences). This rule could also be expressed in the form: follow your own interest as long as no foreign interests object; or, maximize your own well-being, if this does not detract from the wellbeing of any other person.

The PD structure is given in terms of the *interest structure* of the interaction situation. $A$'s interest in sitting out as short a term as possible behind bars is best satisfied if $A$ confesses and $B$ does not: [D,C], then follows [C,C], then [D,D] and at last [C,D]. Symmetrically for B: [C,D], then follows [C,C], then [D,D] and lastly [D,C]. These ordinal evaluations can thus be represented by four numbers: '4' for the highest value in terms of subjective preference, '3' for the second and so forth. In order to facilitate the analysis we characterize the consequences, or respectively the collective outcomes, by the corresponding ranks:

| | | B | |
|---|---|---|---|
| | | D | C |
| A | D | 2,2 | 4,1 |
| | C | 1,4 | 3,3 |

Since the prisoners not only have interests, but also moral values and resulting preferences, which via expected utility maximizing guide the actual decisions of the prisoners (according to the model of economic rationality), we have a large number of possible combinations of these other two types of preferences given the *invariant* structure of subjective interests.

Foremost we consider resulting preferences, because this type of preference seems most likely to save the model of economic rationality as the general adequate model for rational decision-making in the face of the cooperation problem.[7] We will examine all possible symmetrical preference structures:

(1) The persons base their resulting preferences on personal interest. One can call such resulting preferences egoistic preferences. They would have the following form:

A: (4,1) > (3,3) > (2,2) > (1,4)
B: (1,4) > (3,3) > (2,2) > (4,1)

These preferences are Pareto-inclusive with respect to the welfare preferences (PRW). The 'tragedy' of the egoists (and the essence of the prisoners' dilemma) is that with these preferences the egoists end up with the (2,2) outcome. Thus, their own interests are not very well served when they form their (resulting) preferences egoistically.

(2) The resulting preferences are strongly influenced by a sense of justice. The outcomes which are ranked in the same position of the in-

[7] The term 'problematic social situations' introduced by Raub and Voss (1986) is defined as an interaction situation characterized by the conflict between outcomes resulting from individually rational behaviour of strategically inderdependent agents and outcomes which are efficient. Since the prisoners' dilemma is the most important case of a problematic social situation, this type of interaction situation is sometimes called a 'generalized prisoner's dilemma'.

terest preference orderings by every individual are given a high priority in the resulting preference ordering, as long as that priority does not conflict with the PRW criterion: circumstances which are Pareto-superior with respect to all the welfare preferences are given an even higher resulting priority. For four possible outcomes, in which three persons can reach the following interest ranks: (2, 2, 2), (3, 3, 3), (9, 9, 1), (4, 4, 2) the resulting preferences according to this model would be: (3, 3, 3) > (4, 4, 2) > (2, 2, 2) > (9, 9, 1). In the prisoners' dilemma:

A: (3,3) > (2,2) > (4,1) > (1,4)
B: (3,3) > (2,2) > (1,4) > (4,1)

With these preferences it is assumed that if from the moral point of view there is no difference between two outcomes, one prefers the outcome which makes oneself personally better off. These preferences, however, do not guarantee collective rationality because with this strong sense of justice, A chooses the non-cooperative behaviour, D, if he assumes that B also chooses D (it is possible that B chooses D since C is not dominant for B). [D,D] is an equilibrium point in this case with respect to these resulting preferences just as it is with respect to the interest preferences, although there is also the additional second equilibrium point [C,C].

(3) Even if a sense of justice is combined with altruism and we get the following resulting preferences:

A: (3,3) > (2,2) > (1,4) > (4,1)
B: (3,3) > (2,2) > (4,1) > (1,4),

the collective rational outcome cannot be guaranteed for the same reasons as described in case (2).

(4) Resulting preferences of a completely opposite orientation to justice-based preferences could be interpreted as the expression of a strong anti-egalitarianism:

A: (4,1) > (1,4) > (3,3) > (2,2)
B: (1,4) > (4,1) > (3,3) > (2,2)

These anti-egalitarian resulting preferences have two (asymmetrical) equilibrium points and thus cannot guarantee collective rationality either.

(5) If, however, altruism supersedes justice in the form of the following resulting preferences (OR preferences)

A: (3,3) > (1,4) > (4,1) > (2,2)
B: (3,3) > (4,1) > (1,4) > (2,2)

the collectively rational outcome is finally guaranteed: the collectively rational outcome is the equilibrium point of the dominant strategies. But some doubt arises as to the inner consistency of these preference relations because (4,1) > (2,2) is neither altruistic nor just, but rather egoistic, while (1,4) > (4,1) is extremely altruistic.

(6) But a purer altruism also guarantees the collective rational outcome in interaction situations of the prisoner's dilemma type.

A: (1,4) > (3,3) > (2,2) > (4,1)
B: (4,1) > (3,3) > (2,2) > (1,4)

The collectively rational outcome is the only equilibrium outcome for these purely altruistic preferences, and for both prisoners C is the dominant strategy.

(7)

A: (3,3) > (1,4) > (2,2) > (4,1)
B: (3,3) > (4,1) > (2,2) > (1,4)

This symmetrical preference structure could be understood, given a cardinal interpretation of interest preferences, as expressing a weakened altruism: if the increase in the interest rank of the other person equals one's own, then the collective outcome which benefits the other person is given a higher priority. If, however, the fall in one's own interest rank is twice as much as the other's increase, then the resulting preferences take into account the individual's interests and give this more extreme other-serving outcome a lower priority. These preferences have an equilibrium point in the outcome [C,C], and they still guarantee collective rationality.

(8) The resulting preferences which correspond to Sen's assurance game have the following form:

A: (3,3) > (4,1) > (2,2) > (1,4)
B: (3,3) > (1,4) > (2,2) > (4,1)

The person with AG preferences will behave cooperatively as long as he can be assured that the other person will behave likewise cooperatively. Then the rational collective outcome [C,C] is an equilibrium point of the interaction situation. But, in addition, the collectively irrational outcome [D,D] is likewise an equilibrium point. Neither of the prisoners has a dominant strategy. In this case, mutual assurance of cooperation is the condition on which collective rationality depends.

The remaining four preference structures are difficult to interpret.

(9)
A: (3,3) > (4,1) > (1,4) > (2,2)
B: (3,3) > (1,4) > (4,1) > (2,2)

These could be interpreted as the ordinal representation of utilitarian preferences, they guarantee collective rationality. The equilibrium point is the dominant strategy (3,3).

(10)
A: (1,4) > (4,1) > (3,3) > (2,2)
B: (4,1) > (1,4) > (3,3) > (2,2)

In this and the following structure there are two equilibrium points: [C,D] and [D,C].

(11)
A: (4,1) > (3,3) > (1,4) > (2,2)
B: (1,4) > (3,3) > (4,1) > (2,2)

The last structure guarantees again collective rationality

(12)
A: (1,4) > (3,3) > (4,1) > (2,2)
B: (4,1) > (3,3) > (1,4) > (2,2)

We will not go into the details of the preference structures which do not satisfy PRW, but a short overview should complete the picture.

The only PRW irrational preference structure which guaranteing collective rationality could be interpreted as masochistic.

(13) Masochistic resulting preferences:

A: (1,4) > (2,2) > (3,3) > (4,1)
B: (4,1) > (2,2) > (3,3) > (4,1)

Self-hate guarantees - like pure (6) and weakened (7) altruism, like the rather oddly motivated OR preferences, and like (9), (11) and (12) - the collectively rational outcome (with respect to the interest or welfare preferences). With respect to the resulting preferences themselves, however, the agent cannot be satisfied: although they assign the outcome in which they personally fare the best the lowest priority in their resulting preference ordering and the outcome in which they personally fare the worst the highest priority, inevitably they both end up in a position in which they fare quite well: (3,3). We may, however, have reasoned a little carelessly when we claim that they cannot be satisfied with the outcome. In one sense they may indeed be quite happy with the outcome (3,3) because this outcome ranks in both of their personal interest preference orderings in the second position. The prisoners' dilemma reproduces itself to a certain extent for masochists on the level of resulting preferences.

(14) The opposite case (sadistic resulting preferences)

A: (4,1) > (2,2) > (3,3) > (1,4)
B: (1,4) > (2,2) > (3,3) > (4,1)

fails, like masochism, to fulfill the condition PRW. Whereas egoism in the prisoners' dilemma was not successful (trying to fare better, the prisoners fare worse than if they had not tried to fare better at all), this preference scheme oriented towards bringing the other as much harm as possible is successful - due to the symmetrical efforts of both parties. But, nevertheless, the equilibrium point [D,D] is collectively irrational in terms of the interest or welfare structure of the situation. The argument that the non-cooperative outcome in this case may not be collectively irrational because, as one is tempted to say, 'they got what they were asking for', overlooks the fact that for the sadists themselves, this outcome is also worse (the sadist would still like for himself that he fare as well as possible) - otherwise one would have to challenge the welfare valuations and we would no longer be dealing with an interaction situation of the prisoners' dilemma type.

The twelve PRW irrational preference structures contain one structure which guarantees collective rationality. This is interesting because PRW irrationality means that the prisoners prefer the Pareto-inferior outcome to the Pareto-optimal (= collectively rational).

Of the interest-irrational preference structures, six cases allow for the possibility of a collective rational outcome, but do not guarantee it:

(15)

A: (2,2) > (3,3) > (4,1) > (1,4)
B: (2,2) > (3,3) > (1,4) > (4,1)

(16)

A: (2,2) > (3,3) > (1,4) > (4,1)
B: (2,2) > (3,3) > (4,1) > (1,4)

(17)

A: (2,2) > (1,4) > (3,3) > (4,1)
B: (2,2) > (4,1) > (3,3) > (1,4)

(18)

A: (4,1) > (1,4) > (2,2) > (3,3)
B: (1,4) > (4,1) > (2,2) > (3,3)

(19)

A: (1,4) > (4,1) > (2,2) > (3,3)
B: (4,1) > (1,4) > (2,2) > (3,3)

(20)
A: (1,4) > (2,2) > (4,1) > (3,3)
B: (4,1) > (2,2) > (1,4) > (3,3)

Four of the interest-irrational preference structures lead inevitably to collective irrationality. Besides sadistic preferences (14) also the preferences:

(21)
A: (4,1) > (2,2) > (1,4) > (3,3)
B: (1,4) > (2,2) > (4,1) > (3,3)

(22)
A: (2,2) > (4,1) > (1,4) > (3,3)
B: (2,2) > (1,4) > (4,1) > (3,3)

(23)
A: (2,2) > (1,4) > (4,1) > (3,3)
B: (2,2) > (4,1) > (1,4) > (3,3)

(24)
A: (2,2) > (4,1) > (3,3) > (1,4)
B: (2,2) > (1,4) > (3,3) > (4,1)

The task of a second-order normative metapreference theory is to determine the morally best ordering of the possible individual resulting preference orderings.

For PD type situations of interaction with ordinal welfare functions, the resulting preference structures can be separated into three types. The first type contains those preference relations which in a symmetrical structure guarantee collective rationality, the second type contains those preferences which allow for collective rationality, and the third type contains those preferences which lead (in a symmetrical structure) inevitably to collective irrationality. Within these three types there are respectively PRW rational and PRW irrational preference relations.

In this model there are thus three possible outcomes of individual rational behaviour with respect to resulting preferences. A strictly outcome-based normative metapreference theory (which Sen apparently has in mind) would not be able to distinguish any moral difference in value within the members of these indifference classes.

All the individual preference orderings of the first type would be better than any particular resulting preference ordering of the second or the third type, and those of the second type than any of those of the third type. At least to this extent one should consider the idea of a normative metapreference theory to be successful: we have found a method of strictly outcome-based moral evaluation of individual preference relations. But the euphoria of success disappears when one takes a closer look at this moral evaluation of preferences: in the first priority grouping of the moral metapreference scheme one does not only find such preference types as the honorable altruistic preferences (6) and (7), but also the PRW irrational masochistic preference relation (13), and a whole group of completely implausible preference structures, including (9), (5), and (12). In the middle moral group one finds preference structures such as (2) and (3) which intuitively seem to be morally superior to some of the preference relations which the moral metapreference scheme ranks in the highest priority grouping. Also in the middle group are the preferences which take predominant consideration of one's own interests (8), and finally a large number of preference structures (six out of ten) which are PRW irrational and therefore should not be recommended at all. In the group which is given the lowest ranking by moral metapreferences one finds, as expected, the egoistic preference structures, the PRW irrational sadistic preferences, and additionally, four quite implausible PRW irrational preference structures (21), (22), (23), (24).

The concept of an outcome-oriented moral metapreference scheme could appear to some degree convincing (even though the theory generates interpretation problems which have been discussed above) when the analysis is limited to a small group of seemingly adequate examples. But if one considers the particular outcomes in relation to all the possible symmetrical structures of resulting preferences, it becomes clear that collective rationality cannot be secured by maximization with respect to morally recommended preferences. The conflict between individual rationality and collective rationality, thus, is obviously not resolvable by an outcome-oriented change in preferences conceived to guide behaviour via maximization.

## 5. Driving the Wedge between Choice and Value

Traditionally, there are two questions for ethical debate:
1. What is worthwhile, to which goals should people devote their efforts, which life is good?
2. Assuming we know what is good, which action is then correct?

The general attitude both in the classical ethical tradition, as it was founded by Plato and Aristotle, as well as in the economic theory of rationality is that the second question can be trivially solved once the answer to the first question is known - for economic theory this amounts to maximizing preference fulfillment, that is - under risk - maximization of expected utility. The opposing thesis defended in this chapter can be stated as follows: the answers to the second question are mostly independent from the answers to the first question: an answer to the first question does not make the answer to the second question trivial.

Although the considerations above have shown that collective rationality cannot be guaranteed by new kinds of preferences, we have not yet offered a well-defined theory of collective rationality itself. Clearly collective rationality is *not* the rationality of a group as an agent: any conception of collective rationality should be compatible with methodological individualism.[8]

Collective rationality is to be defined based on a 'collectively better'-relation: a collective action $a$ as an $n$-tuple of individual actions is *collectively irrational* if and only if there is another collective action $a'$ which is collectively better than $a$. It is reasonable - at least within a subjectivist context - to postulate Pareto-inclusiveness of any 'collectively better'-relation, therefore any collective action which is not Pareto-efficient is also collectively irrational. This is only a negative criterion of collective rationality, but for the following considerations of practical reason (predicate: $p$-reasonable) it is not necessary to have a positive criterion.

Whereas collective rationality is an attribute of *collective* action, practical reason is an attribute of *individual* action. But there is a close

[8] Cf. Tuomela (1984) ch. 2 and 12, and Kliemt (1986b).

relation between collective rationality and practical reason. *Practical reason requires that individual actions fit into a system of rules of behaviour which the agent rationally can accept.* The main, but not exclusive subject of practical reason is coordination of individual actions. Although we do not assume that coordination of individual actions is a sufficient criterion for moral rightness, it is at least a necessary criterion, and there is hope that with some further qualifications which go beyond the relation to collective rationality, practical reason could be made into a sufficient criterion for moral action.

Certainly a fully developed theory of practical reason would consider not only personal interests and subjective valuations, but also rights, dispositions and virtues of the interacting persons. Personally, I believe that the method of defining practical reason on the basis of these parameters should be contractarian,[9] but for the present purpose we can limit our analysis to subjective preferences. Within this limited analysis, there is a close relation between collective rationality based on personal interests or (subjective) welfare functions and practical reason: any system of rules of behaviour has to allow for collective actions which are collectively rational. So we have a negative criterion for practical reason: one should never act in such a way that there is no system of rules of behaviour in accordance with collective rationality[10] allowing that act.

In the 'small world' of the prisoners, i. e. a world where there are no *external effects* with moral relevance for the situation, the collective action as a combination of uncooperative individual actions [D,D] is definitely collectively irrational. Therefore, in the 'small world' it is *not* in accordance with practical reason to act uncooperatively, i. e. to confess.

Now, there are different possibilities of actions which are in accordance with practical reason: (1) one could 'invent' institutions which influence the prisoners' behaviour. It could be *p*-reasonable to introduce sanctions which would prevent the prisoners from confessing. The prisoners themselves might under certain circumstances vote for such sanctions out of their own personal interest (Hobbes' solution). (2) It could be *p*-reasonable to change one's own subjective valuations

---

[9] Cf. Nida-Rümelin (1987, 1988).

[10] I.e. which under any circumstances does not allow a collective action which is collectively irrational.

to escape the PD situation (Shaftesbury solution). But even these changed subjective valuations can in general not eliminate PD situations - and thus in these remaining cases there is again a need for practical reason. But even more importantly, as the discussion above has shown, there is no plausible subjective valuation which guarantees collective rationality as the result of maximization. So in cases where no Hobbesian solution is possible the Shaftesbury solution for both of the above reasons does not seem to be sufficient either.

What remains is the 'solution' which we call 'Kantian': the prisoners act *p*-reasonably - after the above characterization of practical reason it is clear that this would be a solution. With the Kantian solution the individual behaviour could no longer be characterized as (individually) maximizing the agents' preference fulfillment. There is no subjective valuation, which is maximized by Kantian agents.[11] We do not assume that the Kantian solution is the empirically most widespread, but there is some evidence that the Kantian solution is not only possible for human agents, but that it is in fact empirically relevant.[12]

---

[11] To avoid misunderstandings it may be useful to emphasize that nevertheless it is possible that also Kantian agents maximize some 'utility function' guaranteed by metrification of the preference relation given certain conditions i. e. the von Neumann-Morgenstern axioms (cf. chap. 10, sec. 5). But these formally maximized utility functions represent neither subjective motivations nor subjective values. These utility functions would represent no axiological judgements of the agents concerning the outcomes of the interaction situation, instead these functions would be merely formal representations of the agents' actual behavioural preferences.

[12] Cf. the empirical studies, e.g. Rapoport/Chammah (1965) and Kern/Räder (1987).

CHAPTER 9

# The Plurality of Good Reasons and the Theory of Practical Rationality

## 1. The Theory of Practical Rationality as a Theory of Good Reasons

An action is *rational*, if there is a good reason to perform it. The theory of practical rationality is a theory of good reasons for action.

In our world-life language we speak of reasons not only in *normative*, but also in *descriptive* contexts. One can criticize an action by saying: 'He had no reason to do this'. But one can also utter a purely descriptive statement by saying: 'She did that for the following reason'. One can refer to reasons for action in order to characterize merely the subjective motives of the agent lacking any evaluative connotation, but one can refer to reasons for action also in order to distinguish the right action. The philosophical conceptions of *internalism* and *externalism* originate in an ambivalence of our everyday language.

World-life reasons for action, be they normative or descriptive, are always prima-facie reasons. 'To have a reason for doing *x*' is an elliptic way of expressing that (in the normative sense) one specific aspect of the decision situation (which is said to be the reason for the respective action), *together with* given circumstances and certain presupposed background assumptions (which also include normative and descriptive theories), made this action seem obligatory (normatively) or that this specific aspect of the decision situation etc. was the motive of the agent (descriptively).

'Why did you close the window?', 'Because there was a draught'. The motive to stop the draught was the (descriptive) reason for the agent to close the window. Firstly, however, we can doubt whether this was the real reason for the action of closing the window. 'In reality you did not want anybody to listen to our conversation.' Secondly, even if we (descriptively) accept the motive to stop the draught as the real reason for the action of closing the window, we can still (normatively) reject it, denying it to be a good reason, taking e. g. the view that in these high temperatures a draught is just refreshing and cannot do any damage to one's health. Thirdly, we could also deny the motive to stop the draught in an *indirect way*, taking into consideration implicit background assumptions of the agent which could be proven to be wrong. We could, for example, find out that the draught was not coming from the open window, but from the open door.

Reasons as we use them in our everyday interactions and conversations are only rarely or never a sufficient justification for our actions. To give a reason for an action means to single out one specific aspect of the decision situation which in one or another way plays a particular rôle. This particular rôle might be that the person who asks for the reason for an action is given some information she did not have before and which is necessary to show the action to be justified. A (pragmatically) *successful* justification of an action is brought about, if the person who justifies her action and the person who asks for the justification have a sufficiently similar background knowledge, such that the reason which is given for the action, that is one specific aspect of the decision situation, for both persons justifies the action. An *objectively good* justification is brought about, if the reason given for it would convince an ideally rational person.[1]

In many cases it is a specific aspect of the decision situation which motivates a person to perform a certain action. All other aspects - particularly concerning spontaneous decisions - become less relevant, they are not present in the person's mind. Research in cognitive psychology has shown that our perceptual system immediately registers unusual events and - after a check of relevance - stores them for longer than just in the short time memory. The evolutionary advantage of this particular capacity is obvious: under normal circumstances we react in the usual way, exceptional things, on the other hand, sometimes require different, 'non-usual' ways of behaviour. Actions are the steering instrument of our behaviour. The term 'action' includes a cognitive component. The fact that we single out certain specific aspects in decision situations does not mean that the other, less relevant aspects do not play any rôle at all. Even if they are not each as such and simul-

---

[1] As the concepts of justification and rationality are closely linked, this characterization of an objective justification might at least seem to be circular. Only a more detailed characterization of the content of good reasons can give it more substance.

taneously present in the person's mind, they have before been 'checked' and only then - after having been found to be of no further interest - forgotten again. To give a reason for an action often means to refer to the aspect of a decision situation which was the trigger for an intervening control, that is to intervene with an action into the stream of behaviour. Even if it might be determined to a large extent by dispositions formed during the evolutionary process, this selective procedure is not totally out of the rational control of the agent. He can for example decide to increase his attention, and in doing so he will refine his selection.

Generally, science begins with distinguishing individual cases and with drawing up typologies. Important material for the subject we are concerned with here has been contributed by speech act theory. Speech acts are constituted by systems of norms which in many cases provide reasons for doing something. A person who has made a promise under normal circumstances has a good reason to perform at the given time that action which fulfills the promise. This is not meant in a descriptive sense. These institutions (like promising) have a normative force. We are obliged to do what these institutions tell. This interpretation does not exclude that there are more basic normative rules and principles which allow to reconstruct the more phenomenological normative force of these institutions. To be asked to do something gives a good reason for doing it as we have seen in the discussion of the case in which I have a good reason to pass the salt to my neighbour because she asked me to pass it (cf. ch. 1, sect.2). The evidence of this prima facie rule of obligation is not weaker than e. g. the one of the principle of utility maximization. Even more if there is a conflict between the principle of utility optimization and the principle to respond cooperatively in cases like this, the more abstract principles seem to have the weaker status. Modern reductionist theories of practical rationality therefore have to be corroborated in confrontation to these phenomenological normative rules and not the other way round.

It is a good reason for action to do something because one promised it or because one had been asked for it. In my opinion this is not only *empirically* true as an element of an *internal* description of an institutional fact, but it also seems to be *normatively* true - hence the qualification of this reason for action as a 'good' one. If somebody should convince me that it also meets my personal interests or the aggregate interest of everybody or some other qualified evaluation of the consequences to do what one promised or had been asked for, then this might intensify my conviction that having promised or having been asked for are good reasons for acting - but this information does not *replace* my conviction that having promised or having been asked for something are good reasons for action. The reduction of all possible reasons for action to just *one single* type, i. e. consequential reasons for action can only be attained by deviating from the established practices of justifying actions in our life-world. Having been asked a favour would then no longer be a genuine prima facie-reason, but only an appearent reason for doing something which, under certain conditions, will refer to another, totally different type of reason for action which then, in turn, would rightly become action-guiding. A theory of practical rationality which opposes the greatest part of generally accepted good reasons for action needs a specific justification. I cannot see from where or from what such a theory could get such a justification, since it would have to be strong enough to overcome central and extensive parts of the system of our normative beliefs. Neither do I see any possibility for this, nor - what is more important - any necessity.

## 2. Types of Practical Reasons

We do not get any further in the theoretical clarification by leaving our system of normative beliefs, developing a coherent and perhaps axiomatically structured system *ab ovo* based on the putative solidity of a new fundament. In the descriptive sphere this bold project of philosophical rationalism has since long lost any but historical interest, and hopefully its days are counted in the normative sphere, too. The 'reality shock' of applied ethics seems to have a considerable share in this. However, there is an astonishing delay to general methodological insights finally gaining influence in philosophical ethics as well. Rationalism in the sense of the deduction of knowledge from self-evident propositions (or axioms) still plays a central rôle in ethics inspired by Kantianism as well as by utilitarianism. The rationalistically stimulated overemphasis on the aspect of justification opposes the capitulation of institutionist[2] ethics in the face of the plurality of good reasons. Whereas ethical theories influenced by rationalism[3] regard our life-world moral convictions in the end as worthless for finding and criticizing an ethical position, institutionist ethics restricts itself to the description of established, norm-constituted institutions. Between the rationalistically inspired abolition of the life-world plurality of good reasons on the one hand, and its purely descriptive reconstruction on the other hand, there is room for an adequate theory of practical rationality.

A first step towards a theory of practical rationality is to distinguish different structural types of good reasons. First of all there is the vast field of consequential reasons. A person who wants to change the state of the world in a specific way has reason to perform an action which has the respective desired causal (or probabilistic) consequences. Some theories hold that among all possible consequential reasons there is only one type which represents a good reason: the one referring to the optimization of the subjective state either of the agent herself or of other persons concerned by the action or, more generally, of any animated being concerned by it.[4] In the context of the discussion of the practical syllogism this is sometimes also called the intentionalist model of practical rationality.[5] It seems indeed to be reasonable to assume that good reasons result from a further specification of the general scheme 'I want to have *x*, action *h* is a good means to attain *x*, therefore I choose to do *h*'. Further specifications can then for example refer to what can be reasonably wanted and to a more precise definition of the relation between means and their end. If one wants to keep this scheme, it is, however, important to avoid a consequentialist reduction: The 'I want' does not necessarily solely refer to the consequences of my actions for the future course of the world, but it can also refer to past

---

[2] The common term 'institutional ethics' would be misleading, as it rather refers to the ethics of institutions. An ethical theory which in its normative criteria is based on intuitions is called 'intuitionist ethics', the term 'institutionist ethics' is to be understood analogously.

[3] Cf. ch. 1.

[4] The first type is represented, at least implicitely, by the decision-theoretic model of Savage (1954), the second one is represented by a specific type of utilitarianism.

[5] Cf. v. Wright (1963). Later, v. Wright has given up the intentionalist approach in favour of supplementary 'imperativist' and 'normative' reasons for action, cf. v. Wright (1979).

events, e. g. to obligations I have already taken on or to favours I have been asked before. Generally, however, it is not possible to translate these determinative reasons of our will into preferences over states of the world. The intentionalist scheme can only be maintained if one gives up its consequentialist standard interpretation.

Therefore, to differentiate between consequential and non-consequential reasons for actions is no decision for or against their intentionalist reconstructability. Under normal conditions the fact to have given a promise is a good reason to keep that promise; this reason may sometimes distinguish an action which has consequences which for the agent (or even with respect to a universal standard) are optimizing, but, nonetheless, this optimization is not the reason for keeping the promise. To have given a promise is, generally, a non-consequential reason for keeping it. But I choose an action which fulfills the promise, because I have at this point in time the *intention* to keep the promise, and I choose this action because it is an *adequate means* to realize this intention. This description is compatible with the fact that the causal (and probable) effects of the respective action might not be desired. It may indeed be that from the agent's point of view the state of the world, after having realized this action, is worse than the state of the world which there would be if she had chosen another action instead. Still, keeping a promise is as a rule not irrational, and yet the subjective valuation standard is not wrong. Among non-consequential reasons for action there are reasons which refer to the social rôle of the agent. One can e. g. justify an action with one's parental responsibility for one's children or with specific duties of one's job in the civil service, etc. Reasons of this kind are, generally, not reconstructable as consequential reasons. This is connected with the fact that duties implied in a social rôle do not transmit themselves to an expected subjective valuation of states of the world of the respective person herself. A civil servant has the duty to refuse the bribe offered to him, even in case the expected state of the world after taking the bribe would not only be subjectively better, but would even from a universal point of view be preferable to the present state. Transfers of this kind are typically offered in situations in which the service offered and the service in return conjointly lead to a Pareto-better state. The civil servant would achieve a better (financial) state if he took the money; the person who offers the bribe would, for instance because of accelerated administrative proceedings, have advantages which prevail the disadvantages of her spending the money for the bribe; other persons would so far not be involved. The civil servant who refuses the bribe must not necessarily believe that the state of the world which would follow from this transfer would be worse than the present state. He does not accept the bribe, because taking it would not be compatible with his official duties. The mere reflection on the possible consequences of taking the bribe can already be regarded as a breach of these official duties.

Reasons for action which result from *obligations* taken on also are, as a rule, non-consequential. This type of reasons for action is different from the type of reasons based on duties in that it is constituted only by a *preceding action* of the person herself.

Finally, there are reasons for action supplied by rules which have an action-guiding effect *independent* from our *social rôles* and from *obligations taken on*. We talk of *principle-guided reasons for action*. To save a person from drowning, e. g., is an action which is founded on the principle to help other people in their need. Principle-guided reasons also are generally non-consequential, especially those which refer to individual rights - whereas the promotion of the general welfare, on the other hand, is no principle established in our life-world. The idea to reduce the plurality of good reasons to this one single principle which is not even established in our life-world seems to be just one of those admirable naivities that sometimes come over philosophy. But still, even if this reduction is erroneous, there would remain a certain feeling of uneasiness if we took that as an argument to restrict ourselves just to a mere recognition of the plurality of good reasons. Theoretical comprehension as well as our normative judgment require coherence. Even if the three categories of good reasons we have discussed above were exhaustive and disjoint, little would be gained for a coherent theory of right acting. Preservation of complexity is one thing, to capitulate in face of it is another.

Theories establish connections between propositions. They have to be tested against those elements of our belief system which we are not willing to give up in favour of a theory. Our life-world descriptive beliefs do not need any theories to be regarded as guaranteed. Generally, we trust in what we see; the statement 'The sun is shining' does not need any justification that goes further than our mere judgment by appearances. Nonetheless the way of talking about direct and indirect knowledge is misleading, because it introduces a dichotomy where speaking of different grades in a continuum of more or less direct propositions is more adequate. These general features of our belief systems and their dynamics also characterize our normative beliefs. There are more or less direct reasons for actions. Just as it is rational to assume by mere appearances that the the sun is shining, an action is directly justified if it fulfills a given promise. And just as there might be 'intervening evidences', e. g., if I realize that those mere appearances I relied on were the product of a skillfully arranged deceit, there might also be a case in which another 'intervening' reason is a good reason not to fulfill the promise. Our descriptive as well as our normative theories are based on what directly appears, and on this basis they try to clarify other realms to which we have only indirect access. We try to make our descriptive and our normative convictions coherent with the help of theoretical links. The plurality of our empiric evidences is not abolished by theory, but gets integrated into a theoretical framework. Correspondingly, an adequate normative theory will not abolish the plurality of good reasons, but will embed it in a theoretical frame. In the concluding section of this chapter I want to show how this could be done, taking as an example cooperative reasons for action.

## 3. Cooperative Reasons

In the *narrower sense cooperative reasons for action* refer to collective actions which have these characteristic features: each of the potential agents has an individual interest in the realization of the collective action; if other persons contribute their part to its realization, it would be more advantageous for each of the potential agents not to do her share in it. In this situation a person has a good (cooperative) reason to contribute to the collective action, although, independent from the contribution of other persons, it would be better for her personally not to contribute to this collective action. The approval of a collective action offers even then a good reason to contribute to it, if this doing her share in it does not optimize the consequences for the individual contributing person herself. *Cooperative reasons for action are, per definitionem, non-consequential reasons*. If each person has a good reason to look after her own interests, cooperative reasons for action integrate these prima-facie reasons into a normative theory of collective action which then, in its turn, can become action-guiding for each individual person. Cooperative reasons for action are therefore based on preceding 'primary' reasons.

A slight extension of this concept of cooperative reasons, including not only primary reasons which are determined by personal interests, but also to other, among them genuinly morally determined types of primary reasons, allows to encompass a plurality of situations of interaction. If e. g. a specific type of social interaction is approved of by the individual, not because it optimizes respective personal interests, but because it guarantees the individual rights (e. g. human rights) of all persons involved, then acting in accordance with this structure can be understood as cooperatively justified in the wider sense. This explains, e. g., why persons with a democratic attitude also support the rights, let us say, of their political rivals. From my point of view the state of the world could be better, if some people were restricted in their right of free expression of opinion. Nonetheless one can at the same time, without becoming incoherent, want that this right is preserved, because one can, on the basis of genuinly moral reasons, prefer that system of social interaction where the right of free expression of opinion is guaranteed to any other system where this would perhaps not be the case.

The method of cooperative reasons for action can even be applied in the case of a conflict between different fundamental moral beliefs. If moral beliefs are extremely divergent, it is difficult to find collective actions which can be generally approved of and which can therefore offer to all persons involved a good reason to contribute their part to the respective collective action. Nonetheless there are - so to speak 'on the next higher level' - possibilities of coordination even in the case of extremely divergent fundamental moral beliefs. These coordinations of a higher order typically find expression in principles of tolerance. Cooperation results in this case from obeying to general rules which have as their object the restriction of conflicts between different moral world views. The concept of (secondary) cooperative reasons is here once again applied on *moral world views* which on their part provide primary reasons.

Cooperative reasons for action are not always effective, they are often superseded particularly by primary reasons for action. It is in fact a difficult question for the normative theory under which conditions cooperative reasons can become good reasons for action, that is, under which conditions they should become action-guiding. It would certainly be inadequate to prescribe cooperative behaviour in every prisoners' dilemma situation.

The approach of cooperative reasons for action cannot only be applied to situations of *interpersonal interaction*, but can also be employed to the action coordination of one single person, i. e. in the *intrapersonal case*. Against this background the way of speaking of duties against oneself gets a new sense. The respective optimizing actions - whether the optimization criterion be guided by personal interests or not - would make up a form of life which would not conform to the underlying primary reasons. The postulate of cooperation is also valid for any single person who wants to organize her life in a reasonable way. Cooperation integrates different primary reasons, with that it shapes - interpersonally - the *form of society*, and - intrapersonally - the individual *form of life*. The normative theory of practical rationality can fulfill one part of its systematizing task in developing criteria of cooperation, thus integrating the plurality of good reasons into a theoretic normative context. Theoretical integration often demands modification, in this case the modification of our primary reasons. In this way the theory of practical rationality obtains its critical normative competence.

CHAPTER 10

# Structural Rationality and Coherentism

## 1. Self-control as Orientation Towards Structural Rationality

Structural irrationality of individual behaviour patterns can only be rectified by a specific form of self-control. This can be illustrated using an ordinary, simply-structured example: a long-standing smoker asks himself whether he ought to give up smoking. The smoker's subjective valuations are such that the time integral of his value function increases monotonously the sooner he gives up smoking. The valuation does not only include the smoker's expected general state of health (a probabilistic estimation), but also the pleasure he undoubtedly enjoys in smoking a cigarette, possibly it also includes the damage the smoke of his cigarettes does to other people, etc. If he still does not give up smoking, his case seems to be a clear instance of 'akrasia' or weakness of the will: weighing up all different evaluative aspects, he knows what would be the best thing to do, but he still cannot get himself to do it. This interpretation, however, is not conclusive. It might just as well be the case that the smoker acts *consequentially rational*, if he does not give up smoking - despite the fact that the time integral over his valuation function increases monotonously the sooner he gives it up. The reason for this is that he - as a consequentialist person - is (under normal circumstances) never confronted with the decision to give up smoking. 'Under normal circumstances' here means that we assume him not to have any possibilities of binding himself, neither in the indirect way given by self-chosen sanctions, or by submitting to physical constraint. Normally the smoker who knows that giving up smoking early maximizes his subjective values is only confronted with the question whether during one particular day he ought to smoke or leave it - actually he is only confronted with the question whether he ought to light the next cigarette or not.

Let us have a closer look at these *pointwise* alternatives: as always in a consequentialist weighing up it is first of all necessary to estimate and to assess the causal consequences and the probability distribution of future courses of the world. To renounce smoking today is of a certain, be it only a minimal advantage for the smoker's health. In exchange he will suffer quite a lot today - as everybody knows, the first day without cigarettes is particularly hard. Of course the weighing up must be made for the long term: the decisive factors are not the momentary, but the long-term advantages for the smoker's health. It might happen, therefore, that at the first day of his renunciation the long-standing smoker's state of health really deteriorates. But even this one single day without cigarettes will still be advantageous for his health, even if he continues to smoke the very next day. Perhaps the smoker's bad state in the first day of his abstinence leads to serious consequences regarding his private life: bad mood, disputes, thoughtless remarks, insult. But here, too, we must not only look at what happens in this one single day, but also consider the long-term consequences: with a certain probability the disputes of this day might lead to a permanent discord, but they might just as well resolve old, repressed conflicts. The details of this hypothetical drama are not interesting here; what is important is the answer to the following question: can we, if the saldo of this (L) consequentialist estimation turns out to be negative, nonetheless keep to the premise that giving up smoking sooner is more advantageous for the smoker? The answer is 'yes'.

In order to understand this it is sufficient to apply the consequentialist decision criterion without any restrictions. It is obvious that the long-term consequences of this *one single* day without cigarettes depend on what happens after that day. Let us suppose that the smoker continues to smoke the very next day. Then, even in consideration of long-term consequences, this one day might have brought more frustration than advantage to the smoker. The wording 'in consideration of long-term consequences' must not be misinterpreted: here, we are talking about the long-term consequences of abstinence from smoking on *one particular day*, we are not weighing up the advantages and disadvantages of a long-term renouncement of smoking. If, on the other hand, the smoker continues not to smoke after this day, it might just as well be that the advantages for his health gained in this one day do not offset the disadvantages of the very first day of his renouncement. Between these two possible cases there is a variety of further possibilities - a temporary abstinence from smoking for one month, etc. - which do not bring in essentially new aspects. This argument implicitely uses the principle of dominance. The application of this principle presupposes that the probabilities of the circumstances which are relevant to the estimation of the consequences of an action are action-independent. This premise which characterizes the self-justification of the smoker who tries in vain to fight his addiction to cigarettes can be made explicit in the following way: 'Whether I smoke today or whether I don't is of no relevance for the probability that one day I will definitely give up smoking.' Under this condition, the principle of dominance is applicable. At every single day it is therefore pointwise consequentially rational to continue to smoke.

If, however, we consider only the following alternatives: from today onwards the smoker definitely gives up smoking, from tomorrow onwards the smoker definitely gives up smoking, from the day after tomorrow the smoker definitely gives up smoking, then the first of these alternatives can still *ceteris paribus* have the best consequences. The problem of a consequentialist person is that in general these alternatives are not subjected to decision: a consequentially rational person must make *every single decision* in such a way that its consequences are optimal. There is no doubt that on any single day the smoker can decide whether to smoke or not. He can even decide in every single case whether to light the cigarette or not - except this action should already have become so dispositional that it can no longer be considered an (intentional) action. But from a structural point of view not every series of single pointwise consequentially rational actions is rational, too: perhaps there is another behaviour pattern which in comparison to this series of pointwise consequentially rational actions would increase the time integral of the value function. In the example of the smoker such structurally more advantageous behaviour patterns which would not necessarily be composed of singular consequentially rational decisions would be: 1.) from today onwards the smoker definitely gives up smoking, 2.) from tomorrow onwards the smoker definitely gives up smoking, 3.) from the day after tomorrow onwards the smoker definitely gives up smoking, etc. - in this order.

Self-control can consist in choosing pointwise one's respective actions in such a way that they conform with a desirable structure of one's acting. Self-control in this sense is one way to realize structural rationality, without any change in the range of given options. Another form of self-control is the restriction or modification of the given range of options.[1] This indirect (meta-) strategy is another way to realize structural rationality.

Self-control does not exclusively aim at the restriction of structure-breaking consequences of consequentially rational actions - in many cases it performs other tasks. One of these functions can be the preservation of a person's consistency: I presume that in a particular future situation my personal preferences (advantages, value functions) might change. Therefore I take precautions which either prevent these changes in my subjective valuations, or which exclude that these changes will find expression in respective actions - and these precautions I take are independent of any consequentialist criteria. Nastassja Filippowna's decision (in 'The Idiot' by Dostoyevsky) not to see prince Myschkin any more is an example for the first case; Ulysses, on the other hand, who lets himself be tied to the mast in order to listen to the song of the sirens, is an example of the second. Another function of self-control is the prevention of irrational action: I am afraid of behaving irrationally - in particular, in a weak-willed manner - in a situation I am expecting. My subjective valuations remain unchanged. Now I can either take precautions that this particular situation I am expecting will never occur, or, if it occurs, I can, e. g. modify it by self-chosen sanctions such that it will no longer provoke the behaviour I am afraid of.

If the smoker asks a friend to make sure that he will no longer have any opportunity to get hold of cigarettes, he excludes certain options for actions, but at the same time gains a new one: the option for the action to deprive himself of the possibility to smoke. The decision for this option is pointwise consequentially rational, particularly when the smoker must start from the assumption that he always behaves pointwise consequentially rational. A rational consequentialist person deprives herself of particular optional decisions exactly because she knows that her actions are pointwise consequentially rational. From this argument the Kantian thesis that teleological ethics is incompatible with the freedom of the individual gets new, and in this form unex-

---

[1] The different possibilities and techniques of individual and collective *self-binding* - which is only one out of a variety of possibilities of self-control - are shown in many facets by J. Elster. But there is one crucial difference: Elster discusses self-binding under the aspect of the prevention of *irrational* actions, whereas we are here concerned with the prevention of the structure-breaking effects of *consequentially rational* actions.

pected confirmation. This, however, must not lead to the assumption that a rational consequentialist person is weak-willed - this is just what, *per definition*, she is not: a rational consequentialist person always does what regarding the given value function is optimal: she fulfills all conditions required by the consequentialist theory.

The example of the smoker has the merit of showing very clearly the structural problem of individual agency in the framework of consequentialism. On the other hand it has the disadvantage that its quite complex assumptions are - at least intuitively - not immediately plausible. Let us therefore look at another, shorter example: in general, threats (or less particular: announcements of certain actions which are disadvantageous to another agent, and intendend to compel him to cooperate) expressed by a consequentially rational person are implausible. It is a typical feature of threats that their realization just then ceases to be consequentially rational when the conditions for their realization are given. If it was consequentially rational to realize a threat, the well-informed agent addressed by it (who thinks himself and all other persons to be consequentially rational) would anyway expect it to be realized - an 'additional' verbal expression of the threat would therefore be quite useless. If we assume that there are situations in which the plausibility of a threat is advantageous for the person whom the threat is addressed to, then a consequentially rational person must be interested in not being considered a consequentially rational person. And if we further assume that it is difficult and stressful to keep the orientation of one's own actions secret, then a consequentially rational person has no interest in being consequentially rational. Here, as opposed to the example with the smoker, interaction is involved. But in this example, too, we have nonetheless remained within the context of an analysis of the intrapersonal problem of coordination: we have exclusively concentrated on the question whether a consequentially rational person, as an individual, attains her respective goals. The answer is 'no' - and this is a serious argument against the consequentialist conception of rationality.

## 2. Descriptive and Normative Justifications

Questions like 'Should I do this or that?' or 'Why have you done this?' are questions which ask for reasons for action: Which reasons are there to do this rather than that? Which reasons are there to justify what has been done? The corresponding *philosophical* question is: What is a good reason for the realization of an action?
An example:
A: Why have you changed your bank?
B: Because the bank to which I have changed over pays higher interests.
A: Why do you want higher interests?
B: Because I want to increase my income.
A: Why do you want to increase your income?
B: (It can be supposed that now at the latest, B begins to get impatient and that his answer might be): Because I want it, that's it! Or: That goes without saying, doesn't it?

But even if B remains patient, he will come to a point at which he will no longer be able to give a real answer to A's why-questions. The chain of reasons that can be offered to justify his action has come to an end. In this case this having come to an end of the chain of reasons manifests itself in the reference to a personal interest. But this does not necessarily have to be so.

Perhaps B answers to the last question: 'I want to lay aside some savings for my children which will help them to become economically independent when they are grown-up.' This motive cannot simply be described as a 'personal interest' of B - except in the hypothetical case that it would be advantageous to B if his children, when grown-up, became economically independent as soon as possible. And if B answers to the last question: 'I want to give this money to the Red Cross', this reason for his action does, under normal circumstances, certainly not express a personal interest of him. Nonetheless, this answer can be a suitable justification for his decision.

For A, the answers B gives also are a kind of *explanation* for B's decision to change the bank (in the following we will call this decision/action E). If A had already known before B's decision that B reflected about the question of how to increase his income, A would possibly have *predicted* that B was going to change the bank. At least the *a priori*-probability which A attributes to decision E is less than the probability which A would have attributed to it on the basis of this additional information. In general, however, A will not understand the explanation of E by subjective action goals as a *causal explanation*, because he knows that B is not by a natural law forced to do what optimally corresponds to his goals. In other words: A assumes that B could also have acted in another way. In which sense does A accept the answers of B as a justification of E? In any case, the fact that B's answers give an explanation of E is not a sufficient condition to make them at the same time a justification of E.

If B in consideration of his subjective goals has made an optimal decision, A is not compelled to admit that B should have changed his bank. This would mean that A would have to accept B's action goals, taking into account all possible side effects and value aspects: A would have to agree that B attained the goals he has expressed in his answers. In a situation like the one in the example this will mostly be the case. But this must not cover the fact that the expression of a normative (detached) ought-sentence includes further, additional assumptions which do not refer to the subjective action goals of B. Without such additional assumptions the expression of personal action goals can only supply subjective reasons, i. e. reasons which in our example help the hearer (here: A) to understand (or to explain) why B has decided in this and not in another way. To this type of justification of actions and decisions (which in the following will be called *subjective* justification) corresponds the *descriptive* use of ought-sentences.

To the other type of justification (which in the following will be called objective justification) corresponds the *normative* use of ought-sentences. A successful justification of this second type leads hearer A to say: B ought to do E. For this B's action goals do not necessarily have to be of a moral kind. An objective justification can refer to subjective action goals as well.

The difference between a subjective (descriptive) and an objective (normative) justification of actions and decisions can also be elucidated in the following way: a descriptive justification allows for the deduction of (genuine) ought-sentences only *in the first person*. One can imagine to say to oneself: 'I have the one and only goal Z, and H is the only possibility to attain Z, so I should do H.' A normative justification, on the other hand, also allows the deduction of (genuine) ought-sentences in the third person: 'He has these desires or goals; he should attain these goals - he should do H.' It should be noted that this interpretation is compatible with the theory of the naturalistic fallacy.

### 3. Non-consequentialist Reasons for Actions

Let us discuss another example:

A: Why did you take part in this peace-demonstration?
B: Because I am against any further arming with nuclear missiles.
B: Why are you against a further arming with nuclear missiles?
A: Because in the case of an international crisis they would have a destabilizing effect.
B: And what objections do you have to that?
A: I want peace to become more secure, I do not want it to become more insecure.

One feature that this example and the one above have in common is that, in the end, the reason B gives for his decision refers to his personal attitude. Therefore, we can also in this example distinguish an objective (normative) from a subjective (descriptive) justification: in both examples, B's last answer is a retreat to subjective reasons. Only if the hearer can accept this action goal, he can also accept these answers as an (objective) justification for this decision.[2]

One of the differences between the two examples is that in the second one B is morally motivated, which is not the case in the first one. But this difference is not of interest for us here. There is another difference regarding the *logical relationship between the action goal and the action itself*. In the first example the action chosen by B (changing the bank) is (or is at least conceived to be) a suitable means to attain his goal. In the second example, on the other hand, it seems to be quite improbable that B by taking part in the peace demonstration will attain the disarmament of nuclear missiles. It is likely that not even the probability of disarmament will be increased by his action. Yet this *form* of a justification of an action is not at all unusual: 'Why do you not take the car to go down town?' - 'Because I think the city should be

---

[2] 'Accept' must here be understood in the weak sense of 'to agree that the agent attains his goals'.

kept free from private traffic.' Even if the decision not to use the car for going down town does not keep the city free from private traffic, this answer seems to be a reasonable justification.

The philosophical answers to the question how a decision or an action can be justified differ with respect to the statements they admit as justifications of actions, but they can also be distinguished regarding the relation they presuppose between such justifying statements and the action itself. A justification of an action with the argument that this action is an appropriate means to attain the goals of the agent is a *consequentialist justification.* Whereas the first example includes this kind of consequentialist justification, the arguments which justify the action in the second example *do not have a consequentialist character*. According to the consequentialist point of view subjective reasons for actions are always motivating intentions which refer to particular causal consequences of the respective action. These causal consequences are neither rules nor actions, but states of the world ('states of affairs').

Let us have a look at classical utilitarianism. According to utilitarian theory, an action is well-justified if it maximizes the total utility. This is an objective (not a subject-centred) criterion. But at the same time this theory claims to give a definition of the ideal moral person. In the sense of classical utilitarianism, the motivating intentions of the ideal moral person are directed towards the maximization of total utility. The theory of what is right and just is here transferred to the theory of legitimate reasons for actions. It restricts the range of morally acceptable subjective reasons for actions.

To what extent consequentialist theories, too, must include a certain degree of universalizability, is a question which is still philosophically disputed. If consequentialist reasons for actions are understood normatively (and not descriptively), then they are also bound to the logical necessity of general validity. In the borderline case a high degree of universalizability only admits strictly consequentialist reasons for actions.[3] To attenuate the demand of universalizability means to allow reasons for actions which in the opposite boderline case can also

[3] Even Hare in his (1963) and (1981) maintains that the rules of universalizability logically necessitate an act-utilitarian ethics.

refer to any subjective preferences,[4] given that they fulfill the coherence conditions of theory T1.[5]

In the preceding chapters we have shown that due to several reasons a consequentialist conception of practical rationality is inadequate. This analysis still needs to be completed. If reasons for actions generally were consequential reasons, it would be difficult to maintain a non-consequentialist theory of practical rationality - except one could agree to renounce of the principle of constructivism. If normative theories are always also understood in the sense of a decision procedure, then there must exist, besides consequential reasons for actions, other kinds of reasons for actions as well

In the second example, B does not give a consequentialist justification of his action, because his motivating intentions do not refer to causal consequences of his action. The causal consequences of B's action are not element of his action goals. Are non-consequential reasons, like those in the second example, only fictitious reasons, due to an unprecise way of speaking? Or are there, besides the consequentialist model, other models for the justification of actions?

What we have called the 'consequentialist model of justification' is often named differently, e. g. the 'intentional' or 'teleological model of justification'. But it is indispensible to clearly distinguish 'teleological' on the one hand, and 'consequentialist' on the other hand. 'Intentional' is ruled out, because it evokes the impression as if there were other models of justification that referred to non-intentional actions. G. H. v. Wright had for many years been one of the most exposed representatives of a consequentialist theory which claimed to be universal. But since the end of the 1970s v. Wright allows non-consequentialist models of justification to be equally valid. In the following we will take up some of the considerations of v. Wright, though we can neither adopt his terminology nor his specific interpretation in the sense of 'inward' and 'outward' determinants.[6]

We will first examine the case of the justification 'in the first person', i. e. justifications which only claim subjective validity. We distinguish three forms of subjective justifications:

---

[4] This corresponds to the so-called 'normative interpretation' of decision theory.

[5] See ch. 4.

[6] Cf. v. Wright, (1979), ch. 2.

(1) 'I am preparing a sandwich because I am hungry.'
(2) 'I close the window because my wife asked me to do so.'
(3) 'I will join a cycling tour because I have promised to do so.'

In all three statements the proposition which follows after 'because' justifies the respective action.

(1) fits well into the consequentialist model of justification. My goal is to attain a physical state in which I am not hungry any more. To prepare and to eat a sandwich is an appropriate means to attain this goal. If, however, I am on a diet and if I am, therefore, decided not to eat the sandwich I have prepared, the analysis becomes more complicated. Then (1) would probably be understood as an outline of a causal explanation, not as a justification.

In comparison, (2) and (3) can under normal circumstances certainly not be regarded as consequentialist justifications, because in both cases there would have to be a subjective goal assumed to be attained by the respective action. Which goal do I want to attain by closing the window? Do I want to avoid discord or do I want to please my wife? Such kinds of action goals may sometimes be involved, but normally they do not motivate my action of closing the window. Even the formulation: 'I close the window because I want to do my wife a favour' sounds rather strange. In this example it is not my goal to do my wife a favour, but I do her a favour by closing the window, and I close the window because I have been asked to close it. In general the reference to the fact that I have been asked to close the window is sufficient to justify this action. With v. Wright we call this an *imperativist* justification.

The justification in (3), on the other hand, is again of a different kind. Here, too, it does not seem to make sense to look for an action goal which is assumed to be attained by this action, even if there do exist cases in which this would be appropriate. It is for example possible, that nonwithstanding the bad weather I take part in the cycling tour for the only reason that I fear my friends would otherwise be disappointed. They would be disappointed because I had promised to come. In this respect it would be appropriate to say: 'I will come because I have promised to do so.' But then the fact that I have given a promise is not the real reason for my taking part in the tour. The real reason is that I do not want my friends to be disappointed, and my promise only plays the rôle of a (causal) determinant of this disappointment. But normally the fact that I have promised to take part in the cycling tour is the primary reason for me to come. There may of course be other aspects which prevent this reason to become effective, but the simple fact that I have promised to do $x$ is a reason to realize $x$. With v. Wright we call this second, non-consequentialist type a *normativist* justification.

A consequentialist theory of practical rationality would only be adequate if every adequate justification of an action was reconstructable within the theoretical framework of consequentialism. But in subjective justifications, obviously reasons for actions play a part which cannot be consequentially reconstructed.

We still have to examine whether these results are exclusively restricted to subjective (descriptive) justifications. In consequentialist justifications the transition from a subjective (descriptive) to an objective (normative) justification is characterized by the fact that the action goals of the agent are acceptable (can be accepted by the respective hearer). There is an analogy in non-consequentialist justifications: in (2) the hearer will then form a (detached) ought-judgment, 'he ought to close the window', if he (like the speaker himself) thinks it to be appropriate to do this kind of favour. In (3) the same is true of the institution of promise. In this respect, we can conclude, nothing changes in comparison to subjective models of justification: even in a normative conception there are justifications which cannot be reconstructed consequentially.

Particular attention must be given to the fact that *objective* justifications - independent from the question whether they are based on consequential,[7] imperativist or normative reasons for actions - always include a form of *generalization*. An objective (normative) justification follows the structure of a *first characterization of the concrete action*, its *subordination* under a more general description of the action, and finally (when the process of the formation of the justification comes to its end) the *approval of an action criterion* - which is nothing else but the approval of one type of action. A person who justifies an action in the face of a critical audience generalizes the description of this action and tries to meet general approval *by describing* the action *in a particular way*. Which kinds of description can be used largely depends on

[7] Consequential reasons are those which according to the consequentialist point of view are the only adequate reasons to justify an action.

the totality of the respective action-guiding, motivating and preceding intentions and on the circumstances under which the action is or was realized. The difference between consequentialist and non-consequentialist justifications is expressed in the character of the type of action in which the respective chains of justification come to their end.

According to a consequentialist theory T an action is well-justified if it can be described as an action which maximizes the expected value with regard to the value function over the states of the world postulated by theory T. To maximize the expected value is a characteristic feature of actions. With the moral law, Kant has named another distinctive feature of actions: the normative justification ends where the action in question is described as being in accordance with the moral law. There is an important parallel in these two theories: both justification models are based on the distinction of one specific justifying type of action: only those actions which belong to this type are well-justified. In both theories, the distinction of this one type of action also has the status of a warrant: actions of this type are warranted. But it must not (in the spirit of the classical conception of axiomatic theories) be concluded that this distinction could not itself again be made an object of critique. Some elements of the critique of the consequentialist model of justification have been shown in this and in the preceding chapters.

The power of consequentialism and Kantianism is due to the fact that they are both able to identify and to characterize one single justifying type of action, whereas our everday language and the normative institutions which structure our actions of every day always refer to a great variety of different justifying types of action. Both theories reduce this variety to one single, simple criterion. This, however, is not only the source of their power, but also the weak point of both theories. The critique of consequentialism does not automatically mean to warrant its antipode in the history of ideas: from a systematic point of view consequentialism and Kantianism have far too many things in common.

## 4. Coherence Without Consequentialism

In chapter 2 we have distinguished two theories of practical rationality: T1 and T2. The ideal rational person regarding T1 has a (subjective) valuation function $u$ ('utility') over all possible states of the world (out of $X$) and a subjective probability function ('believing') over all sets of states of the world. Her actions maximize the expected value of $u$ with regard to $p$. The ideally rational person with regard to T2, on the other hand, is defined by the condition that her preference relation fulfills the coherence axioms. T1 and T2 are not equivalent. T2, however, guarantees the existence of a - linear transformation excepted - definite valuation function which represents the person's preferences. The theory of practical rationality which demands of the ideally rational person that she intentionally chooses her actions in such a way that she maximizes the expected value of the (subjective) utility of their consequences we have called 'Bayesian consequentialism'.

The arguments we have developed have shown that Bayesian consequentialism is not a convincing theory of practical rationality. Even moral qualifications of the valuation of the consequences did not change this result. Still unclarified, however, are the implications for the coherence axioms of T2. T2 can be regarded as the nucleus of a coherence theory of practical rationality. Therefore, not only consequentialism, but also the coherence theory of practical rationality is at our disposal. T2 cannot be used to warrant T1, because T2 does not imply T1. But still there remains the disturbing question: which rôle does the valuation function constituted by T2 play? What is optimized, when the rational agent with regard to T2 maximizes this function? Which relation is there between this function and the agent's subjective preferences? In this section we want to answer these questions.

Imagine an ideal Kantian agent who orientates his action preferences - at least in so far as moral, not pragmatic questions are concerned - to the fulfilment of the moral law (the categorical imperative). Let us further suppose that he is a 'sensible' Kantian agent who in situations in which obeying the categorical imperative would lead to disastrous consequences, chooses an action which is not compatible with the categorical imperative. For the following it is sufficient to assume that the categorical imperative sometimes recommends actions of which the consequences do not maximize the expected value regarding the agent's subjective valuations of states of the world. Sometimes the

Kantian agent will decide in favour of actions which have consequences that (even moral valuations included) are not optimal (or - in the probabilistic case - do not bring about the maximal expected value). Can the preferences of this Kantian agent fulfil the conditions of the coherence theory of practical rationality (T2)?

The answer is: *If X is the set of states of the world, and if preferences over actions are identified with preferences over probability distributions over X assigned to these actions, then the decision behaviour of the Kantian agent is not, as a rule, compatible with the coherence conditions of T2.*

This can easily be understood: an action $h$ and an action $h'$ can both result in the same probability distribution over states of the world, but at the same time $h$ might be allowed, whereas $h'$ might be prohibited by the categorical imperative. For a simple fact the classification of an action within the preference relation of the Kantian agent does not only follow the probability distributions over consequences (or states of the world) induced by this action, but is also based on the conformity or deficiency of the action with respect to a certain criterion (the categorical imperative). With this, however, the axioms of substitution, continuity and monotony - which means all essential coherence conditions of T2 in a probabilistically enriched set of alternatives - are not compatible. This result is only valid, though, if the above formulated presupposition is given: 'If $X$ is the set of states of the world, and if preferences over actions are identified with preferences over probability distributions over $X$ assigned to these actions'. This presupposition can in short terms be described as the assumption of the *representability of actions by probability distributions over states of the world.*

The incompatibility of the coherence theory and Kantian rationality is removed, however, if one gives up this form of coupling actions to states of the world. The coherence of preferences *of actions* (which allows a simultaneous attribution of degrees of believing or presuming and desirability) is fundamental to the coherence theory of rationality, anyway. It is therefore only consistent to examine the coherence of the Kantian agent's action preferences without loading this examination with the interpretation 'actions are represented by probability distributions over states of the world'. The alternatives which are to be classified within the agent's preference relation are now options. We therefore have to examine whether *the Kantian agent's preferences over options fulfil the conditions of the coherence theory of practical rationality.*

Suppose that $X$ is the set of options and $X^*$ is the set of prospects over such options. Prospects over $X$ must be interpreted in the sense that - according to the respective circumstances - together with an action $h$ another action $h'$ or another action $h''$ etc. is realized at the same time. E. g.: I switch on the water pump. Depending on the respective circumstances this action can either mean to provide the residents with drinking water, or to poison them. In the second case I would have, in switching on the water pump, simultaneously realized another action - poisoning the residents. No prospects over actions can be assigned to concluding actions, they must therefore be directly classified within the agent's preference ordering. This is analogous to actions in the case of certainty in which a state of the world is a certain consequence of a respective action.

Can the preferences of the Kantian agent over a thus interpreted set of alternatives $X^*$ be coherent in the sense of T2? For technical and pragmatic imperatives in the Kantian sense this is in any case valid. But even if the realization of an action is weighed up with respect to a moral point of view, the coherence conditions, applied to preferences over options for actions, do not necessarily conflict with the rule to act exclusively according to a maxim which one can at the same time want to become a general law.[8]

It can be supposed that the Kantian agent, too, is indifferent between two prospects, if they can be transformed into one another by means of a mathematical transformation according to the probability calculus; therefore the condition of reduction is fulfilled. We can further suppose that the Kantian agent, too, if he is indifferent between an $x$ out of $X$ and a prospect $a$, can always substitute $x$ by a, without any change in his respective preferences; therefore the condition of substitution is likewise fulfilled. If the Kantian agent is confronted with two prospects which both have probabilities that refer to the same pair of actions, then he will prefer that proposal which includes a higher probability for the action he prefers:

[8] Cf. Kant, *Grundlegung zur Metaphysik der Sitten*, AA 421.

$$\forall x,y \in X:\left[x > y \rightarrow \left(p \geq p' \rightarrow \langle p/x\&(1-p)/y\rangle \geq \langle p'x\&(1-p')/y\rangle\right)\right]$$

therefore the condition of monotony is fulfilled as well.

Some problems arise, however, with the condition of continuity. In the first place because, if talking about the 'subjectively best state of the world' already is a sort of challenge to the imagination, talking about a 'subjectively best action' is certainly beyond comprehension in general, and even more so in the framework of a non-axiological ethics of duties; secondly, because the classification within the preference relation of actions which have to be judged from a moral point of view brings about some difficulties.

Let us first examine the case of a purely moral dichotomy: actions are morally allowed or morally prohibited, depending on whether their maxims conform to the criterion of the categorical imperative. There is no moral hierarchy of actions. The moral law takes the first place superior to all other kinds of pragmatic or technical kinds of valuations of actions. Actions commanded by the moral law have absolute priority: if two different actions could be realized, but only the first of them is commanded by the moral law, whereas the second is not, then the first one must be chosen, however positive the consequences of the second one might be. The priority of actions commanded by the moral law does not as such infringe the condition of continuity. It is at a first sight simply irritating that all actions commanded by the moral law do not only have absolute priority, but that there is also indifference between them. In a categorical interpretation of this priority the principle of continuity is violated, however: suppose that $h_1$ is commanded by the moral law (i. e. $\neg h_1$ is morally prohibited and does not conform with one's duties), whereas $h_2$ and $h_3$ are morally allowed. Further suppose that the agent, starting from a pragmatic point of view, prefers $h_2$ to $h_3$. This constellation is possible only if together with $h_2$ or $h_3$ at the same time $h_1$ is realized, too - in so far, as in weighing up the alternatives, it is only $h_2$ and $h_3$ which must be taken into consideration. (If the realization of $h_2$ or, respectively, of $h_3$ did not at the same time necessarily involve the realization of $h_1$, $h_2$ and $h_3$ would both imply the realization of a morally prohibited action, that is $\neg h_1$, and this would contradict our assumption.) In any case, the best action is the one commanded by the moral law, whereas the worst one is the morally prohibited. Morally allowed actions imply actions commanded by the moral law. Therefore there cannot exist any prospects which have as a good result an action commanded by the moral law, and as a bad result a morally prohibited action which is at the same time indifferent to a morally allowed action.

In the categorical version of Kantian ethics the idea of a continuum within the valuation of actions, of which the higher part includes actions commanded by the moral law, while the lower part includes actions that are morally prohibited, and of which the part in the middle includes actions that are morally allowed, cannot be maintained. But formally the condition of continuity is not infringed: in the context of a moral estimation the premise of the condition $x_a > x > x_z$ cannot be met; therefore, in a trivial sense (*ex falso quod libet*) the condition of continuity is fulfilled. Nonetheless it must be noticed that in the open interval (0,1) there is no probability $p$, such that $p / x \;\&\; (1 - p) / z = y$, in which $x$ is an action commanded by the moral law, $z$ is a morally prohibited, and $y$ is a morally allowed action. An amoral (pragmatic) estimation which necessarily already presupposes an action to be morally permitted does not allow an integration of the moral and non-moral point of view, either - but within an amoral estimation there is no reason to assume that the condition of continuity is not fulfilled.

Only a 'consequentialist attenuation' of Kantian morals which allows us to weigh up conformity with the rule on the one hand, and consequences of actions on the other hand, and which - against Kant - e. g. also permits lying, if with a lie the life of an innocent person can be saved, would make it possible to apply the principle of continuity and would therefore also facilitate a coherent numerical representation of action preferences. The violation of the condition of the generalizability of a maxim could then be offset by very good consequences of an action or by the prevention of a disaster. In the sense of supererogatory actions even the moral sphere would include different degrees: not only the conformity with the moral law, but also e. g. the contribution to human welfare would define what is morally desirable. We can summarize this modification in the term *consequentialist attenuation*. Actions which follow maxims that one can want to become a general law could then be coherently classified within the preference relation, *qua* consequentialist attenuation they would be representable by a simultaneous attribution of a belief function and a desirability (or value) function.

But even a consequentially attenuated conception of Kantian ethics still excludes the transition from the coherence model to the consequentialist model of optimization. Both essential conditions for this transition cannot be realized: *In the first place because it is not possible to assign probability distributions over states of the world to actions, and secondly because* u *as a quantitative representation of preferences over actions cannot be interpreted as a representation of the motives for the respective action. The attribution of quantitative values to elements out of* X* *only represents the coherent preference relation over actions; it does not represent the subjective desirability of states of the world.*

Here we have used the term 'states of the world' in the usual sense because it is of course possible to 'formally' assign to actions probability distributions over states of the world, if the description of these states includes statements like 'the action of the person fulfilled the categorical imperative'. With this modification, however, the valuation function constituted by the coherence model could no longer be transferred into the consequentialist model of optimization, because then it would be no longer states of the world which would be optimized, but an intrinsic value would be assigned to certain features of the action itself.

To act out of respect for the moral law is a possible reason for an action. As we have shown above, this reason for an action is on certain conditions (consequentialist attenuation) compatible with - as we would like to call it - *Ramsey*-coherence: a person's preferences can be Ramsey-coherent, even if they are not motivated by the optimization of consequences. They can also be Ramsey-coherent, if the reason for the respective action is just 'the moral law'.

## 5. Form of Life and Form of Community

In the course of our discussion the heuristic distinction between questions of rationality and questions of morality could not be upheld. This becomes especially clear in the context of the transition to intrapersonal considerations: the fact that consequentialist optimization leads to destroying structures not only constitutes a problem for cooperation in a society but also for the individual design of one's life. While in classical Greek and Roman philosophy the question for the good design of one's life was regarded as the most important ethical problem, there has been little philosophical interest in this question since the rise of early modern philosophy until today. Several problems which approaches in modern philosophical ethics are facing seem to be a result of this. One outstanding example of this is the consequentialist approach to moral philosophy, i. e. the use of an economic paradigm of practical rationality in ethics.

It is legitimate to assess an ethical theory by analyzing the properties which a society of humans would have if it were composed solely of humans which cope with the normative criteria of this ethical theory. In the ideal consequentialist society the shaping of an individual life faces internal and external demands: the *external demands* are due to the consequentialist call to take into account all forseeable consequences of ones actions including the effects of these actions for other people's actions. These external demands render reasonable planning of life under normal circumstances impossible since they undermine the pursuit of individual goals and projects as well as the maintenance of personal bonds.[9] The *internal demands* of consequentially rational agency destroy the structures of the individual plans of life due to the pointwise optimization.

Summarizing the results presented, we can label the core of our critique as the *twofold* (interpersonal and intrapersonal) *coordination problem of a consequentialist conception of practical rationality*. Coordination arises by a reasonable embedding of individual (pointwise) actions in certain structures of actions. Consequentially rational agency, however, does not lead to desirable structures of individual and social behaviour.

The two core notions of ethical discourse, the concepts of a *good life* and of a *well-ordered society* are interrelated in a complex manner which cannot be accounted for by a consequentialist approach.[10] It is

---

[9] See my (1993b), ch. 9 and 10.

[10] The classical theory claiming that justice and good life coincide - as e. g. presented in Plato's *Gorgias* - surely is too optimistic. However, here the problem is articulated while the modern schism of good life and moral duty constitutes an avoidance of the problem.

true that the consequentialist theory of practical rationality covers - depending on the utility function - the spectrum ranging from self-oriented optimization to individual self-sacrifice for the common good. However, our analysis has shown that this theory is not convincing at any point of this spectrum. Consequentialism comes to grips with both tasks of a theory of practical rationality only in an insufficient way: nor does it offer viable criteria for designing individual lives or for the reasonable coordination of social agency and individual forms of life.

The straightforward reaction facing the problem of coordination in a framework of consequentialist rationality is to constrain the set of options. If there are fewer alternatives to decide among then in many cases there is less chance of deciding wrongly. This is the core of different practises of self-binding as well as of establishing sanctions *in foro externo* or *in foro interno*. In the consequentialist framework there is a tradeoff between more rationality and less freedom of choice. If rational individuals have to wish not to be able to decide (rationally) then this is an argument against the corresponding theory of rationality.

The form of life is largely formed by the structures of individual and pointwise agency. These structures which to a certain degree are chosen individually determine the quality of individual forms of life as well as the form of society as a whole, the latter of which can be thought of as a netlike structure consisting of individual forms of life woven together through different forms of interaction.

A possible motive for action is *coordination*: to act individually and pointwise so that the individual action is embedded in an endorsed structure of individual or social agency. The prisoner in his dilemma can have the motive to act in a way he wants the other prisoner to act as well. The *motive of coordination* (and especially cooperation) can be a good reason for a decision. An adequate theory of justifications for actions should not exclude this specific type of *normative reasons*. There is, e. g., the phenomenon of coordinative intentions which are formed in certain situations of interaction and which can be reconstructed in the following way: some member of a group has a *coordinative intention* if he wants to contribute his part to a collective action insofar as he can expect every well informed and rational member of the group to act in the same way.[11] Coordinative intentions can also

[11] For details see Tuomela, (1984), ch. 4, and Nida-Rümelin (1986), pp. 96-108.

refer to the design of an individual life: I act pointwise in the way which is in accordance with the form of life most preferred by me.

There is again a structural relation among different structures of actions: individual structures taken together form structures of greater generality - individual forms of life are structurally linked to a form of society. If one does not regard the individual person as a conglomerate of momentary sensations, perceptions and reactions,[12] then she is the carrier of the intrapersonal structuring of her (pointwise) actions and of the coordination of individual forms of life with those of other persons. The moral person is situated - metaphorically speaking - at the edge between two different levels of coordination.

The structures of actions are neither intra- nor interpersonally predetermined *in toto* (by education, sanctions, conventions, anthropological determinants etc.) but rather in large parts subject to free decision - they can be formed, developed, changed or kept. We are therefore facing a twofold task: to develop criteria for morally desirable structures[13] and for the embedding of individual actions in these structures[14] - the consequentialist theory of practical rationality and the ethical theories relying on it cannot account for these tasks.

---

[12] See the contributions in Elster (1986).

[13] This comprises, under an interpersonal aspect, *inter alia* the axiological theory of social institutions and under an intrapersonal aspect the theory of good forms of life.

[14] In the course of two and a half millenia much has been thought and written with regard to the relation between self-love and reason, *viz.* justice which could enrich the contemporary debate on practical rationality. Just to take two examples from many, cf. on the one hand the second letter of Alexander Pope (1733) in which the author starts by saying that man has a natural interest in others' welfare, and he takes humanity to be connected to a harmonic whole by a 'chain of love'; on the other hand, Duc de La Rochefoucauld (1665) analyzes even apparently altruistic behaviour as being irrational, egoistic and unfree.

# BIBLIOGRAPHY


Abell, P.: 1981, *Rational Choice Theory*, Aldershot.

Allais, M.: 1953, 'Le comportement de l'homme rationnel devant le risque: Critique des postulats et axioms de l'école Américaine', *Econometrica* **21**, 503-546.

Allais, M./Hagen, O., eds.: 1979, *Expected Utility Hypothesis and the Allais Paradox*, Dordrecht.

Anand, P.: 1987, 'Are the Preference Axioms Really Rational?', *Theory and Decision* **23**, 189-214.

Anscombe, G. E. M.: 1957, *Intention*, Oxford.

Anscombe, A. M.: 1965, 'The Intentionality of Sensation: A Grammatical Feature', in *Analytical Philosophy*, ed. J. Butler, Oxford.

Aristotle, *Nicomachean Ethics*, transl. by T. Irwin, Indianapolis 1985.

Arrow, K./Intriligator, M., eds.: 1986, *Handbook of Mathematical Economics*, Vol. III., Amsterdam.

Arrington, R. L.: 1989, *Rationalism, Realism, and Relativism. Perspectives in Contemporary Moral Epistemology*, Ithaca/London.

Arrow, K. J.: 1951, *Social Choice and Individual Values*, New York.

Audi, R.: 1986, 'Acting for Reasons', *Philosophical Review* **95**, 511-546.

Austin, J. L.: 1962, *How to Do Things with Words*, London.

Axelrod, R.: 1981, 'The Emergence of Cooperation among Egoists', *American Political Science Review* **75**, 306-318.

Axelrod, R.: 1984, *The Evolution of Cooperation*, New York.

Barry, B.: 1987, 'Lady Chatterley's Lover and Doctor Fisher's Bomb Party: Liberalism, Pareto Optimality, and the Problem of Objectionable Preferences', in Elster/Hylland (1987).

Becker, G. S.: 1976, *The Economic Approach to Human Behavior*, Chicago.

Beckermann, A.: 1977, *Gründe und Ursachen*, Kronberg/Ts.

Bennett, D.: 1965, 'Action, Reason and Purpose', *Journal of Philosophy* **62**, 85-96.

Bennett, J.: 1973, 'The Meaning-Nominalist Strategy', *Foundations of Language* **10**, 141-168.

Bennett, J.: 1976, *Linguistic Behaviour*, Cambridge.

Bicchieri, C.: 1989, 'Self-refuting Theories of Strategic Interaction: a Paradox of Common Knowledge, *Erkenntnis* **30**, 69-85.

Birnbacher, B.: 1988, *Verantwortung für zukünftige Generationen*, Stuttgart.

Black, M.: 1964, 'The Gap between 'Is' and 'Should'', *Philosophical Review* **73**, 165-181.

Black, M., ed.: 1965, *Philosophy in America*, London.

Brandt, R. B.: 1979, *A Theory of the Good and the Right*, Oxford.

Breyer, E.: 1978, *Das Liberale Paradox. Eine wohlfahrts- und spieltheoretische Untersuchung*, Meisenheim.

Brink, D.: 1989, *Moral Realism and the Foundations of Ethics*, Cambridge.

Brinkley, R. et al., eds.: 1971, *Agent, Action and Reason*, Oxford.

Broad, C. D.: 1930, *Five Types of Ethical Theory*, London.

Broad, C. D.: 1950, 'Egoism as a Theory of Human Motives', *Hilbert Journal*, **48**.

Broome, J.: 1991, *Weighing Goods*, Oxford.

Butler, J.: 1726, *Fifteen Sermons Preached at the Rolls Chapel*, ed. W. R. Matthews, London 1953.

Campbell, R./Sowden, L., eds.: 1985, *Paradoxes of Rationality and Cooperation*, Vancouver.

Carlson, E.: 1995, *Consequentialism Reconsidered*, Dordrecht etc.

Chernoff, H./Moses, L. E.: 1959, *Elementary Decision Theory*, New York.

Chisholm, R. M.: 1966, 'Freedom and Action', in Lehrer (1966).

Chisholm, R. M.: 1972, 'Sentences about Believing', in Marras (1972).

Chisholm, R. M.: 1981, *The First Person: An Essay on Reference and Intentionality*, Minneapolis.

Condorcet, M. J. A.: 1785, *Essai sur l'application de l'analyse à la probabilité des décisions rendues à la pluralité des voix*, Paris.

Debreu, G.: 1959, *Theory of Value*, New York.

Dennett, D.: 1978, *Brainstorms*, Hassocks.

Dickmann, A./Mitter, P., eds.: 1986, *Paradoxical Effects of Human Behavior - Essays in Honour of Anatol Rapoport*, Heidelberg.

Eberlein, G. L./Berghel, H., eds.: 1988, *Theory and Decision - in Honour of W. Leinfeller*, Dordrecht.

Edgeworth, F. Y.: 1881, *Mathematical Psychics: An Essay on the Application of Mathematics to the Moral Sciences*, London.

Elster, J.: 1979, *Ulysses and the Sirens - Studies in Rationality and Irrationality*, Cambridge.

Elster, J.: 1983, *Sour Grapes - Studies in the Subversion of Rationality,* Cambridge.
Elster, J.: 1986, *The Multiple Self*, Cambridge.
Elster, J./Hylland, A., eds.: 1987, *Foundations of Social Choice Theory*, Cambridge.
Feinberg, J.: 1970, 'Action and Responsibility', in Feinberg (1970a), 119-151, revised in Black (1965), 134-160.
Feinberg, J.: 1970a, *Doing and Deserving*, Princeton/N. J.
Fishburn, P. C.: 1964, *Decision and Value Theory*, New York/London/Sydney.
Fishburn, P. C.: 1966, 'Additivity in Utility Theory with Denumerable Product Sets', *Econometrica* **34**, 500-503.
Fishburn, P. C.: 1970, *Utility Theory for Decision Making*, New York.
Fishburn, P. C.: 1972, *Mathematics of Decision Theory*, Mouton/The Hague/Paris.
Flew, A. G. N., ed.: 1951, *Logic and Language*, Oxford 1951.
Foot, P.: 1962, 'Free Will as Involving Determinism', in Morgenbess/Walsh (1962).
Foot, P.: 1978, *Virtues and Vices and Other Essays in Moral Philosophy,* Oxford.
Frankfurt, H. G.: 1971, 'Freedom of The Will and The Concept of a Person', *Journal of Philosophy* **68**, 5-20.
Gärdenfors, P.: 1979, 'Forecasts, Decisions and Uncertain Probabilites', *Erkenntnis* **14**, 159-181.
Gauthier, D.: 1986, *Morals by Agreement*, Oxford.
Gauthier, D./Sugden, R., eds.: 1993, *Rationality, Justice and the Social Contract*, New York etc.
Gean, W.: 1965/66, 'Reasons and Causes', *Review of Metaphysics* **19**, 667-688.
George, D.: 1984, 'Meta-preferences: Reconsidering Contemporary Notions of Free Choice', *Journal of Social Economics* **11**, 92-107.
Gewirth, A.: 1978, *Reason and Morality,* Chicago.
Gibbard, A.: 1973, 'Manipulation of Voting Schemes: A General Result', *Econometrica* **41**, 587-601.
Göttiner, H. W./Leinfellner, W., eds.: 1978, *Decision Theory and Social Ethics*, Dordrecht.
Grice, H. P.: 1957, 'Meaning', *Philosophical Review* **66**, 377-388.
Grice, H. P.: 1969, 'Utterer's Meaning and Intentions', *Philosophical Review* **78**, 147-177.

Griffin, J.: 1986, *Well-Being. Its Meaning, Measurement, and Moral Importance*, Oxford.

Gunnerson, K., ed.: 1975, *Language, Mind and Knowledge*, Minneapolis.

Hare, R. M.: 1963, *Freedom and Reason*, Oxford.

Hare, R. M.: 1981, *Moral Thinking, its Levels, Method and Point*, Oxford.

Harmann, G.: 1982, 'Moral Relativism Defended', in Krausz/Meiland (1982).

Harris, H., ed.: 1978, *Scientific Models and Man: The Herbert Spencer Lectures*, Oxford.

Harrison, R., ed.: 1980, *Rational Action*, Cambridge.

Harsanyi, J. C.: 1953, 'Cardinal Utility in Welfare Economics and the Theory of Risk Taking', *Journal of Political Economy* **61**, 434-435.

Harsanyi, J. C.: 1955, 'Cardinal Welfare, Individualistic Ethics, and Interpersonal Comparisons of Utility', *Journal of Political Economy* **62**, 309-321.

Harsanyi, J. C.: 1958, 'Ethics in Terms of Hypothetical Imperatives', *Mind* **67**, 305-316.

Harsanyi, J. C.: 1976, *Essays on Ethics, Social Behavior, and Scientific Explanation*, Dordrecht.

Harsanyi, J. C.: 1977a, 'Rule Utilitarianism and Decision Theory', *Erkenntnis* **11**, 25-53.

Harsanyi, J. C.: 1977b, 'Morality and the Theory of Rational Behavior', *Social Research* **44**, 623-656.

Harsanyi, J. C.: 1978, 'Bayesian Decision Theory and Utilitarian Ethics', *American Economic Review, Papers and Proceedings* **68**, 223-228.

Harsanyi, J. C.: 1979, 'Rule Utilitarianism, and Arrow's Impossibility Theorem', *Theory and Decision* **11**, 289-317.

Harsanyi, J. C.: 1980, 'Rule Utilitarianism, Rights, Obligations, and the Theory of Rational Behavior', *Theory and Decision* **12**, 115-133.

Harsanyi, J. C.: 1985, 'Rule Utilitarianism, Equality and Justice', *Social Philosophy and Policy* **2**.

Hart, H. L. A.: 1948/49, 'The Ascription of Responsibility and Rights', *Proc. Arist. Soc.* **44**, reprinted in Flew (1951), 145-166.

Heal, J.: 1978, 'Common Knowledge', *Philosophical Quarterly* **28**, 116-131.

Hegselmann, R.: 1994, 'Solidarität in einer egoistischen Welt - Eine Simulation', in Nida-Rümelin (1994c).

Hirschman A. O.: 1982, *Shifting Involvements: Private Interest and Public Action,* Princeton/N. J.

Hobbes, Th.: 1651, *Leviathan*, London.

Hobbes, Th.: 1658, *Elementorum philosophiae, sectio secunda: De homine*, London.

Hobbes, Th.: 1697, *Elementorum philosophiae, sectio tertia: De cive*, Paris.

Holler, M./Illing, G.: 1991, *Einführung in die Spieltheorie*, Berlin/Heidelberg.

Jeffrey, R. C.: 1965a, *The Logic of Decision*, Chicago.

Jeffrey, R. C.: 1965b, 'Ethics and the Logic of Decision', *Journal of Philosophy* **62**, 528-539.

Jeffrey, R.C.: 1974, 'Preferences among Preferences', *Journal of Philosophy* **71**, 377-391.

Jehle, F.: 1974, *Boolesche Algebra*, München.

Kant, I.: 1785, *Grundlegung zur Metaphysik der Sitten*, Riga 1785.

Kant, I.: 1788, *Kritik der praktischen Vernunft*, Riga 1788.

Kant, I.: 1797, *Die Metaphysik der Sitten*, Königsberg 1788.

Kenny, A.: 1963, *Action, Emotion and Will*, London.

Kern, L./Nida-Rümelin, J.: 1994, *Logik kollektiver Entscheidungen,* München/Wien.

Kern, L./Räder, H.-G.: 1988, 'Private Goods and Public Bads', in Eberlein/Berghel (1988).

Kliemt, H.: 1985, *Moralische Institutionen - Empiristische Theorien ihrer Evolution,* Freiburg/München.

Klein, P., ed.: 1990, *Praktische Logik,* Göttingen.

Kliemt, H.: 1986a, *Antagonistische Kooperation - Elementare spieltheoretische Modelle spontaner Ordnungsentstehung,* Freiburg/München.

Kliemt, H.: 1986b, 'Individualism, Libertarianism and Non-Cognitivism', *Analyse und Kritik* **8**, 211-228.

Kneale, W.: 1968, 'Intentionality and Intensionality', *Arist. Soc. Suppl.* **42**, 73-90.

Körner, S., ed.: 1974, *Practical Reason,* Oxford.

Kondo, T.: 1990, 'Some Notes on Rational Behaviour, Normative Behaviour, Moral Behaviour and Cooperation', *Journal of Conflict Resolution* **34**, 495-530.

Krausz, M./Meiland, J. W., eds.: 1982, *Relativism - Cognitive and Moral*, Notre Dame/London.

Krüger, L./Gärtner, W.: 1983, 'Alternative Claims and Sen's Paradox', *Theory and Decision* **15**, 211-229.

Leach, J./Butts, R./Pearce, G., eds: 1973, *Science, Decision and Value. Proceedings of the 5th Univ. of Western Ontario Philos. Coll. 1969*, Dordrecht.

Lehrer, K., ed.: 1966, *Freedom and Determinism*, ed. K. Lehrer, New York.

Lenk, H., ed.: 1977, *Handlungstheorien - interdisziplinär*, Vol. 1, München.

Lenk, H., ed.: 1979, *Handlungstheorie - interdisziplinär*, Vol. 2, München.

Lewis, D.: 1969, *Convention: A Philosophical Study*, Cambridge.

Lewis, D.: 1975, 'Languages and Language', in Gunnerson (1975), 3-35.

Luce, R. D./Raiffa, H.: 1957, *Games and Decisions*, New York.

Luce, R. D./Suppes, P.: 1963, 'Preference, Utility and Subjective Probability', in Luce/Bush/Galanter (1963), 249-410.

Luce, R. D./Bush, H. R. R./Galanter, E., eds.: 1963, *Handbook of Mathematical Psychology*, Vol. 3, New York/London.

Mackie, J. L.: 1977, *Ethics. Inventing Right and Wrong*, Harmondsworth.

Marras, A., ed.: 1972, *Intentionality, Mind and Language*, Chicago.

Marschak, J.: 1950, 'Rational Behavior, Uncertain Prospects and Measurable Utility', *Econometrica* **18**, 111-141.

McMurrin, S., ed.: 1980, *The Tanner Lectures on Human Values*, Cambridge etc.

McPherson, M. S.: 1982, 'Mill's Moral Theory and The Problem of Preference Change', *Ethics* **92**, 2-237.

Melden, A. I.: 1961, *Free Action*, London.

Mele, A.: 1988, 'Effective Reasons and Intrinsically Motivated Actions', *Philosophy and Phenomenological Research* **48**, 723-731.

Mezzetti, C.: 1987, 'Paretian Efficiency, Rawlsian Justice and the Nozick Theory of Rights', *Social Choice and Welfare* **4**, 25-37.

Milnor, J.: 1954, 'Games against Nature', in Thrall/Coombs/Davis (1954), 49-59.

Morgenbess, S./Walsh, J. J., eds.: 1962, *Free Will*, Englewood Cliffs.

Moulines, C.-U.: 1976, 'Approximate Application of Empirical Theories', *Erkenntnis* **10**, 201-227.

Mueller, D.: 1979, *Public Choice*, Cambridge.

Munier, B.: 1987, *Risk, Decision and Rationality*, Dordrecht.

Nagel, T.: 1980, 'The Limits of Objectivity. The Tanner Lecture on Human Values', in McMurrin (1980), 75-139.

Neumann, J. v./Morgenstern, O.: 1947, *Theory of Games and Economic Behavior*, Princeton.

Nida-Rümelin, J.: 1986, 'Wir-Intentionen und die Logik kollektiver Entscheidungen', *Analyse und Kritik* **8**, 96-108.

Nida-Rümelin, J.: 1987a, *Entscheidungstheorie und Ethik*, München.

Nida-Rümelin, J.: 1987b, 'Der Vertragsgedanke in der politischen Philosophie', *Zeitschrift für Politik* **34**, 200-206.

Nida-Rümelin, J.: 1988, 'Plädoyer für eine kontraktualistische Philosophie der Politik', in Weinberger (1988).

Nida-Rümelin, J.: 1990, 'Der praktische Schluß des Aristoteles und das *revealed preference*-Konzept der rationalen Entscheidungstheorie', in Klein (1990), 203-216.

Nida-Rümelin, J.: 1991a, 'Zur Philosophie der Demokratie: Arrow-Theorem, Liberalität und strukturelle Normen', *Analyse und Kritik* **13**, 184-203.

Nida-Rümelin, J.: 1991b, 'Practical Reason or Metapreferences? An Undogmatic Defense of Kantian Morality', *Theory and Decision* **30**, 133-162.

Nida-Rümelin, J.: 1992, 'Rationale Ethik', in Pieper (1992), 154-172.

Nida-Rümelin, J.: 1993a, 'Practical Reason, Collective Rationality and Contractarianism', in Gauthier/Sudgen (1993), 53-74.

Nida-Rümelin, J.: 1993b, *Kritik des Konsequentialismus*, München.

Nida-Rümelin, J.: 1994a, 'Begründung in der Ethik', *Logos* **3**.

Nida-Rümelin, J.: 1994b, 'Das rational choice-Paradigma - Extensionen und Revisionen', in Nida-Rümelin (1994c), 2-29.

Nida-Rümelin, J., ed.: 1994c, *Praktische Rationalität - Grundlagenprobleme und ethische Anwendungen des rational choice-Paradigmas*, Berlin.

Nida-Rümelin, J.: 1994d, 'Rational Choice: Extensions and Revisions', *Ratio* (New Series) **7/2**, 122-144.

Nida-Rümelin, J.: 1994e, 'Die Vielfalt guter Gründe und die Theorie praktischer Rationalität', *Protosoziologie* **6**, 95-103.

Nida-Rümelin, J.: 1994f, 'Rationality and Morality', in Pauer-Studer (1994), 217-228.

Nida-Rümelin, J./Schmidt, T./Munk, A.: 1996, 'Interpersonal Dependency of Preferences', *Theory and Decision* **41**, 257-280.

Nozick, R.: 1973, 'Distributive Justice', *Philosophy and Public Affairs* **3**, 45-126.

Nozick, R.: 1974, *Anarchy, State and Utopia,* Oxford.

Opp, K.-D.: 1983, *Die Entstehung sozialer Normen - Ein Integrationsversuch soziologischer, sozialpsychologischer und ökonomischer Erklärungen*, Tübingen.

Parfit, D.: 1986, *Reasons and Persons*, Oxford.

Pauer-Studer, H., ed.: 1994, *Norms, Values, and Society*, Dordrecht etc.

Pieper, A., ed.: 1992, *Geschichte der neueren Ethik 2*, Tübingen.

Pitcher, G.: 1960, 'Hart on Action and Responsibility', *Philosophical Review* **69**, 226-235

Pope, A.: 1733, *An Essay on Man. Being the First Book of Ethic Epistels*, London.

Prior, A. N.: 1969, 'Intentionality and Intensionality', *Arist. Soc. Suppl.* **42**, 91-106.

Raiffa, H.: 1978, *Decision Analysis*, London.

Ramsey, F. P.: 1931, 'Truth and Probability', in Ramsey, *Foundations. Essays in Philosophy, Logic, Mathematics and Economics,* ed. D. H. Mellor, Atlantic Highland/N. J. 1978.

Rapoport, A./Chammah, A.: 1965, *Prisoner's Dilemma. A Study in Conflict and Cooperation*. Ann Arbor.

Rapoport, A./Guyer, M. J./Gordon, D. G.: 1976, *The 2 x 2 Game*, Ann Arbor.

Raub, W./Voss, T.: 1986, 'Conditions for Cooperation in Problematic Social Situations', in Dickmann/Mitter (1986).

Raub, W./Voss, T.: 1988, 'Individual Interests and Moral Institutions - An Endogenous Approach to the Modification of Preferences', Paper presented at the Conference 'The Emergence, Maintenance, and Effects of Social Institutions', Werner-Reimers-Stiftung, Bad Homburg.

Riley, J.: 1986, 'Generalized Social Welfare Functionals: Welfarism, Morality and Liberty', *Social Choice and Welfare* **3**, 233-254.

Rochefocauld, Duc de la: 1665, *Reflexions ou sentences et maximes morals*, Paris.

Rothkirch, C. v.: 1981, *Rationales Verhalten im öffentlichen Interesse*, Frankfurt a. M./New York.

Satterthwaite, M.: 1975, 'Strategy-proofness and Arrow's Conditions: Existence and Correspondence Theorems for Voting Procedures and Social Welfare Functions', *Journal of Economic Theory* **10**, 187-217.

Savage, L. J.: 1951, 'Statistical Decision Functions', *Journal of the American Statistical Association* **46**, 55-67.

Savage, L. J.: 1954, *Foundations of Statistics*, New York (2nd ed. New York 1972).

Savigny, E. v.: 1974, *Die Philosophie der normalen Sprache*, Frankfurt a. M.

Scheffler, S.: 1982, *The Rejection of Consequentialism*, Oxford.

Schelling, T. C.: 1978, 'Egonomics', *American Economic Review (Papers and Proceedings)* **68**, 290-294.

Schelling, T. C.: 1980, 'The Intimate Contest of Self-Command', *Public Interest* **60**, 94-118.

Schelling, T. C.: 1984, *Choice and Consequences*, Cambridge/Mass.

Schick, F.: 1971, 'Beyond Utilitarianism', *Journal of Philosophy* **68**, 656-667.

Schick, F.: 1972, 'Democracy and Interdependent Preferences', *Theory and Decision* **3**, 55-75.

Schmeidler, D./Sonnenschein, H.: 1978, 'Two Proofs of the Gibbard-Satterthwaite Theorem on the Possibility of a Strategy Social Choice Function', in Göttinger/Leinfellner (1978).

Schmidt, T.: 1995, *Rationale Entscheidungstheorie und reale Personen*, Marburg.

Schneeweiß, H.: 1967, *Entscheidungskriterien bei Risiko*, Berlin/Heidelberg/New York.

Schüssler, R.: 1990, *Kooperation unter Egoisten*, München.

Searle, J. R.: 1969, *Speech Acts*, Cambridge.

Searle, J. R.: 1982, *Ausdruck und Bedeutung*, Frankfurt/M.

Searle, J. R.: 1983, *Intentionality: An Essay in the Philosophy of Mind*, Cambridge.

Sen, A. K.: 1970, *Collective Choice and Social Welfare*, San Francisco.

Sen, A. K.: 1974, 'Choice, Ordering and Morality', in Körner (1974).

Sen, A. K.: 1978, 'Rational Fools: A Critique of the Behavioural Functions of Economic Theory', in Harris (1978).

Sen, A. K.: 1979, 'Personal Utilities and Public Judgments. Or what is wrong with Welfare Economics', *The Economic Journal* **89**, 537-558.

Sen, A. K.: 1986, 'Social Choice Theory', in Arrow/Intriligator (1986).

Shimony, A.: 1955, 'Coherence and the Axioms of Confirmation', *Journal of Symbolic Logic* **20**, 1-28.

Simon, H. A.: 1983a, *Models of Bounded Rationality,* Cambridge.

Simon, H. A.: 1983b, *Reasons in Human Affairs,* Oxford.

Skyrms, B.: 1992, 'Chaos in Game Dynamics', *Journal of Logic, Language, and Information* **1**, 111-130.

Slote, M.: 1989, *Beyond Optimizing. A Study of Rational Choice*, Cambridge.

Smart, J. J. C./Williams, B.: 1973, *Utilitarianism - For and Against*, London.

Spaemann, R.: 1978, 'Naturteleologie und Handlung', *Zeitschrift für Philosophische Forschung* **32**,. 481-493

Spohn, W.: 1978, *Grundlagen der Entscheidungstheorie*, Kronberg/Ts.

Spohn, W.: 1994, 'Wie läßt sich die Spieltheorie verstehen?', in Nida-Rümelin (1994c).

Stegmüller, W.: 1973, *Probleme und Resultate der Wissenschaftstheorie und Analytischen Philosophie, Bd. 4: Personelle und Statistische Wahrscheinlichkeit*, Berlin/Heidelberg/New York.

Stegmüller, W.: 1977, 'On the Interrelations between Ethics and other Fields of Philosophy and Science', *Erkenntnis* **11**, 55-80.

Stegmüller, W.: 1979, *Hauptströmungen der Gegenwartsphilosophie*, Vol. II., Stuttgart.

Stegmüller, W.: 1979, *The Structuralist View of Theories*, Berlin/Heidelberg/New York.

Steigleder, K.: 1992, *Die Begründung des moralischen Sollens*, Tübingen.

Stoutland, S.: 1970, 'The Logical Connection Thesis', *American Philosophical Quarterly Monograph* **4**.

Suppes, P.: 1973, 'The Concept of Obligation in the Context of Decision Theory', in Leach/Butts/Pearce (1973).

Tanguiane, A.: 1992, *Aggregation and Representation of Preferences. Introduction to Mathematical Theory of Democracy*, Berlin/Heidelberg/New York.

Taylor, C.: 1964, *The Explanation of Behaviour*, London.

Taylor, R.: 1966, *Action and Purpose*, Englewood Cliffs.

Thrall, R. M./Coombs, C. H./Davis, R. L., eds.: 1954, *Decision Processes*, New York/London.

Trapp, R.: 1985, 'Utility Theory and Preference Logic', *Erkenntnis* **22**, 301-309.

Trapp, R.: 1988, *'Nicht-klassischer' Utilitarismus: Eine Theorie der Gerechtigkeit*, Frankfurt a. M.

Tuomela, R.: 1984, *A Theory of Social Action*, Dordrecht/Boston/Lancaster.

Tversky, A./Kahnemann, D.: 1984, 'Choice, Values and Frames', *American Psychologist* **39**, 341-350.

Voss, T.: 1985, *Rationale Akteure und soziale Institutionen*, München.

Wald, A.: 1950, *Statistical Decision Functions*, New York.

Weinberger, O., ed.: 1988, *Philosophie des Rechts, der Politik und der Gesellschaft*, Wien.

Wiesenthal, H.: 1987, 'Die Ratlosigkeit des Homo Oeconomicus', introduction to J. Elster, *Subversion der Rationalität*, Frankfurt/New York, 7-20.

Williams, B.: 1980, 'Internal and External Reasons', in Harrison (1980).

Wriglesworth, J. L.: 1985, *Libertarian Conflicts in Social Choice*, Cambridge.

Wright, G. H. v.: 1963, *The Varieties of Goodness*, London.

Wright, G. H. v.: 1971, *Explanation and Understanding*, Ithaca/N.J.

Wright, G. H. v.: 1977, *Handlung, Norm und Intention*, Berlin/New York.

Wright, G. H. v.: 1977, 'Elemente der Handlungslogik', in: Lenk (1977).

Wright, G. H. v.: 1979, 'Das menschliche Handeln im Lichte seiner Ursachen und Gründe', in Lenk (1979).

Wunderlich, D.: 1976, *Studien zur Sprechakttheorie*, Frankfurt a. M.

# THEORY AND DECISION LIBRARY

## SERIES A: PHILOSOPHY AND METHODOLOGY OF THE SOCIAL SCIENCES

*Editors*: W. Leinfellner (*Vienna*) and G. Eberlein (*Munich*)

1. G. Zecha and P. Weingartner (eds.): *Conscience: An Interdisciplinary View*. Salzburg Colloquium on Ethics in the Sciences and Humanities (1984). 1987 ISBN 90-277-2452-0
2. R.W. Scholz: *Cognitive Strategies in Stochastic Thinking*. 1987 ISBN 90-277-2454-7
3. H. Nurmi: *Comparing Voting Systems*. 1987 ISBN 90-277-2600-0
4. M. Schmid and F.M. Wuketits (eds.): *Evolutionary Theory in Social Science*. 1987 ISBN 90-277-2612-4
5. C.L. Sheng: *A New Approach to Utilitarianism*. A Unified Utilitarian Theory and Its Application to Distributive Justice. 1991 ISBN 0-7923-1301-1
6. F. Forman: *The Metaphysics of Liberty*. 1989 ISBN 0-7923-0080-7
7. G. Bernard: *Principia Economica*. 1989 ISBN 0-7923-0186-2
8. J.W. Sutherland: *Towards a Strategic Management and Decision Technology*. Modern Approaches to Organizational Planning and Positioning. 1989 ISBN 0-7923-0245-1
9. C. Vlek and G. Cvetkovich (eds.): *Social Decision Methodology for Technological Projects*. 1989 ISBN 0-7923-0371-7
10. P. Hoyningen-Huene and F.M. Wuketits (eds.): *Reductionism and Systems Theory in the Life Sciences*. Some Problems and Perspectives. 1989 ISBN 0-7923-0375-X
11. K.G. Grunert and F. Ölander (eds.): *Understanding Economic Behaviour*. 1989 ISBN 0-7923-0482-9
12. G. Antonides: *The Lifetime of a Durable Good*. An Economic Psychological Approach. 1990 ISBN 0-7923-0574-4
13. G.M. von Furstenberg (ed.): *Acting under Uncertainty*. Multidisciplinary Conceptions. 1990 ISBN 0-7923-9063-6
14. R.L. Dukes: *Worlds Apart*. Collective Action in Simulated Agrarian and Industrial Societies. 1990 ISBN 0-7923-0620-1
15. S.O. Funtowicz and J.R. Ravetz: *Uncertainty and Quality in Science for Policy*. 1990 ISBN 0-7923-0799-2
16. J. Götschl (ed.): *Erwin Schrödinger's World View*. The Dynamics of Knowledge and Reality. 1992 ISBN 0-7923-1694-0
17. R. von Schomberg (ed.): *Science, Politics and Morality*. Scientific Uncertainty and Decision Making. 1993 ISBN 0-7923-1997-4
18. J. Baron: *Morality and Rational Choice*. 1993 ISBN 0-7923-2276-2
19. M. Allais and O. Hagen (eds.): *Cardinalism*. A Fundamental Approach. 1994 ISBN 0-7923-2398-X
20. E. Carlson: *Consequentialism Reconsidered*. 1995 ISBN 0-7923-3547-3
21. J. Götschl (ed.): *Revolutionary Changes in Understanding Man and Society*. 1995 ISBN 0-7923-3627-5
22. A. Camacho: *Division of Labor, Variability, Coordination, and the Theory of Firms and Markets*. 1996 ISBN 0-7923-3832-4

23. R. Hegselmann, U. Mueller and K.G. Troitzsch (eds.): *Modelling and Simulation in the Social Sciences from the Philosophy of Science Point of View*. 1996
ISBN 0-7923-4125-2
24. J. Nida-Rümelin: *Economic Rationality and Practical Reason*. 1997
ISBN 0-7923-4493-6

www.ingramcontent.com/pod-product-compliance
Lightning Source LLC
Chambersburg PA
CBHW060745150926
51501CB00003B/92
*9780792344933*